Leckie×Leckie
Scotland's leading educational publishers

#1 FOR REVISION

National 5
COMPUTING SCIENCE
SUCCESS GUIDE

N5 COMPUTING SCIENCE *SUCCESS GUIDE*

Ted Hastings • Ray Krachan

© 2013 Leckie & Leckie Ltd
Cover image © Jetrel

001/23092013

10 9 8 7 6 5 4 3 2

ISBN 9780007504848

Published by
Leckie & Leckie Ltd
An imprint of HarperCollins*Publishers*
Westerhill Road, Bishopbriggs, Glasgow, G64 2QT
T: 0844 576 8126 F: 0844 576 8131
leckieandleckie@harpercollins.co.uk
www.leckieandleckie.co.uk

Printed in Great Britain by Martins the Printers Ltd

Special thanks to
Jill Laidlaw (copy-edit); QBS (layout); Ink Tank (cover design); Donna Cole (proofread); Ruth Hall (proofread)

A CIP Catalogue record for this book is available from the British Library.

Acknowledgements
P46, 47, 55, 56 and 57 Copyright © 2001–2013 Python Software Foundation; All Rights Reserved.

P58–70 App Inventor images
This work is licensed under a Creative Commons Attribution-ShareAlike 3.0 Unported License © 2012-2013 Massachusetts Institute of Technology

P76 Image of Microsoft Access database excerpt used with permission from Microsoft.

P78 Image of Microsoft Excel spreadsheet excerpt used with permission from Microsoft.

All other images are © Shutterstock or © Thinkstock

Contents

UNIT 2: Information systems design and development

Course outline and assessment

Syllabus

The National 5 Computing Science course consists of two units and an assignment, which is made up from content from the two units.

This book presents the content of the two units in a more compact and digestible form than that of a full-blown textbook. However, care has been taken to ensure that both topics have been covered in sufficient depth, to give you a strong position from which to tackle the exam.

Assessment

The grade for the course is determined by the exam and the assignment task. The exam has 90 marks available (60% of total mark), and the assignment has 60 marks available (40% of total mark).

Unit assessment

Both units have a short test at the end. These must be passed for you to complete the course. However, the tests do not contribute to the overall grade of the course.

The exam

The exam lasts for 1 hour 30 minutes, and has a total of 90 marks. Pace yourself through the exam. Try to find a balance between finishing too early, because you have not written answers with enough depth and explanation, and rushing to finish, because you have written answers with too much depth and explanation. Try to write as neatly as you can, this will keep the marker in a better mood than if he/she has to struggle to read your writing. There will be a 50–50 split between the units. The question paper will come in two sections. Section one will have

20 marks and will consist of short answer questions. Section two will have 70 marks and will consist of extended response questions.

Assignment

The purpose of the assignment is to assess practical application of knowledge and skills from the units to develop a solution to an appropriately challenging computing science problem.

Computer programs

Program code

A computer program is a sequence of instructions that tells a computer how to carry out a specific task. You will already have encountered a whole range of computer programs that carry out different tasks.

- **Computer games** are programs that display graphical objects on the computer screen and allow the user to interact with them by means of keyboards, pointing devices and touch screens.
- **Computer applications** are programs that allow a computer user to work with different types of data, for example words (word processors), numbers (spreadsheets) or images (graphics software).
- **Utility programs**, such as anti-virus programs and disk defragmenters, are used to protect a computer against threats and to maximise its performance.

Even the computer's operating system (for example, Windows or Linux) is simply a suite of programs that allows the user to interact with the computer and helps it to manage files, memory, tasks and input-output operations.

You may come across the expression 'program code'. This can have two distinct meanings – source code or machine code.

Source code

The **source code** of a program is simply the program instructions as written by the programmer in a format resembling English. The process of programming is sometimes referred to as 'coding'. The source code is generally entered in text format, using some kind of text editor. The source code for a very simple program (written in Python) to display the words 'Hello World' on the screen would look like this: `print("Hello World!")`

However, this code cannot be directly understood by the computer, so it needs to be converted to machine code before it can be executed.

Machine code

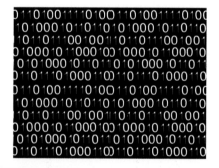

Source code is fine for human readers, but a computer only really understands binary numbers (1s and 0s), so the program needs to be converted to a sequence of 1 and 0 digits before it can be executed. This sequence is known as **machine code**. A single line of source code may produce several lines of machine code.

Assembly language is a more readable version of machine code in which the binary code is replaced by mnemonics, for example, INC for an increment instruction.

EXAM TIP

The **source code** of a program is the sequence of instructions written by the programmer in a programming language. The **machine code** is the same program converted into a binary format that the computer can execute.

Programming languages

There are thousands of different programming languages available. They are sometimes referred to as **high-level languages** to distinguish them from **low-level languages**, such as machine code or assembly language. All programming languages share a number of common characteristics but languages can vary greatly depending on their intended purpose.

New languages are developed regularly while older ones drop gradually out of use. Currently popular programming languages include C and its derivatives (C++ and C#), various dialects of Basic (Visual Basic, True Basic, BBC Basic), Java, JavaScript and Python.

Software development environments

Programming languages are often combined with editors, compilers, interpreters and other tools to form **software development environments**, which can help simplify and organise the software development process. The table below shows some of the different types of environments you might encounter.

Environment	Description	Examples
Graphical	Code is assembled by combining graphical objects which represent instructions, variables and other programming constructs	Scratch Build Your Own Blocks (BYOB)
Games development	Specifically suited to writing computer games	C++, Gamemaker, Greenfoot, Dark Basic
Apps development	Designed for producing applications for mobile devices, such as smartphones and tablets	Java Development Tools App Inventor
Text-based	Text-based programming environments	True Basic, Python

Quick Test 1

1. Which type of program code is written in a format resembling English?
2. Which type of programming language uses mnemonics to represent instructions?
3. Which type of program code is made up of ones and zeroes?
4. What is the name of the suite of programs that helps the computer to manage files, memory, tasks and input-output operations?

Variables

A **variable** is a named location in the computer's memory that can be used to store a value, for example a word or a number.

You may find it useful to think of a variable as a pigeonhole – the location is always the same, but it can store different values at different times. If we want to store someone's surname in the computer's memory we might use a variable called **_Surname_**.

It's important to distinguish between the **name** of the variable and the **value** stored in it. The name will always stay the same, but the same variable can be used to store different values.

Some programming languages distinguish between **variables** and **constants**. The value of a variable can change at any time, but the value of a constant always remains the same.

Variable types

Variables can be of different types. We'll look at these in more detail later, but for now, the most important ones are:

- **String:** a string of characters, such as a word or a phrase, for example 'McDonald' or 'Well done!'. Strings can contain numbers, for example 'Dave12'.
- **Integer:** a whole number, for example 16 or 1024.
- **Float:** a number with a decimal point, for example, 3.14 or 98.6. These are sometimes referred to as **real** or **floating point** numbers.
- **Boolean:** variables of this type can only have the value 'True' or 'False'. We'll see later how they are used.

	Type ▶	STRING	FLOAT	INTEGER
	Value ▶	McDonald	62.5	16
	Name ▶	surname	height	age

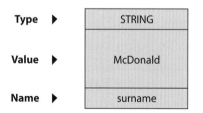
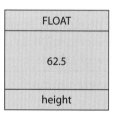
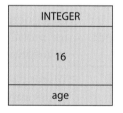

In many programming languages, for example Pascal and C++, variables need to be defined or declared before they are used. In others, such as Python and most dialects of Basic, variables are created automatically the first time they are used.

EXAM TIP

Some common "numbers" are not numbers at all. For example, a "telephone number" can contain dashes, spaces or brackets, so it would be stored as a string variable.

Assigning values to variables

The simplest way to create a variable in Python is to assign a value to it, for example the Python statement

```
Height = 62.5
```

will create the float variable **Height** and store the value 62.5 in it.

This is known as an **assignment statement**. Note that the use of the equals sign (=) is a bit different from its everyday meaning. We are not saying that height **is equal** to 62.5 – we are **making it equal** to 62.5 by storing this value in the variable.

The type of a variable is determined by the value assigned to it when it is created, so

```
Age = 16
```

will create the integer variable **Age** and store the value 16 in it.

Similarly

```
Surname = "McDonald"
```

will create the string variable **Surname** and store the value 'McDonald' in it. Note that we have to put quotes round the value to be stored if we want to store a string.

The type of variable can be changed if a value of a different type is later assigned to it. For example, if we initially wrote **Age = 23** then **Age** would be of type integer. However if we later wrote **Age = "twenty-three"** then **Age** would be of type string.

In Python the names of variables are case sensitive, for example: **surname** and **Surname** are different variables. Keep this in mind when writing programs, as it is easy to make mistakes.

It is possible to assign the values True or False directly to a Boolean variable, but this is seldom done. Boolean variables are usually assigned a value as the result of evaluating an expression as we'll see later.

EXAM TIP

The type of a Python variable is determined by the value initially assigned to it. The type can be changed if a value of a different type is assigned later.

Quick Test 2

1. Which type of variable is used to store words or phrases?
2. Which type of variable can only have the values True or False?
3. A Python program contains the statement **Age = 15**. What type is the variable **Age**?
4. What Python function can be used to convert strings to floating point numbers?
5. How are String values shown in a Python program?

Input and output

Displaying information on the screen

We can display the value contained in a variable by using the **print()** **function**. For example

```
print(Age)
```

would display the current value of the variable **Age** on the screen. We'll look at functions in more detail later. The brackets after the function name indicate that the function needs to be given a value to operate on.

```
# assign values to variables

Surname = "McDonald"
Age = 16
Height = 62.5

# print values of variables

print(Surname)
print(Age)
print(Height)
```

The short program shown on the right assigns values to three variables then prints these values on the screen as follows:

```
McDonald
16
62.5
```

The lines starting with a hash symbol (#) are comments for the benefit of human readers.

We can use a slightly more elaborate version of the **print() function** to provide the reader with additional information about what we are printing, for example:

```
Age = 16
print("The value of age is: ", Age)
```

would print:

The value of age is: 16

Sometimes it is useful to have a bit more control over the format of integers or float values, for example if we want to lay out data in a table. Python offers a vast range of formatting options – two of the simpler ones are shown below.

We can make an integer fill with 0s to a fixed width by using the format attribute:

```
Count = 4
print('{0:03}'.format(Count)}
```

This will display the value of **Count** as 004.

We can also print float values to a specified number of decimal places, for example:

```
Pi = 3.1415926
print("%.2f" % Pi)
```

This will display the value of **Pi** as 3.14.

EXAM TIP

Remember that Python allows us to format integer or float output in a variety of different ways.

Reading information from the keyboard

Another way of storing information in a variable is to use the **input() function** to read it from the keyboard, sometimes referred to as the console. For example, the following short program would ask the user to enter the value of **Surname**, read it from the keyboard and display it on the screen:

```
Surname = input("Enter your surname: ")
print("Your surname is: ", Surname)
```

Values input from the keyboard are always of the string type. If we want to input a value for any other type of variable we need to convert it to the appropriate type. The **int() function** can be used to convert strings to integers and the **float() function** to convert strings to floating point numbers. For example, we can input an integer or float value as follows:

```
Age = int(input("Enter value for age: "))
Height = float(input("Enter value for height: "))
```

EXAM TIP

Remember that in Python, data typed in from the keyboard is always of type string. If you want to make it into any other type you'll need to convert it.

Quick Test 3

1. What Python function is used to display values on the screen?
2. What does a line starting with the hash symbol (#) mean in a Python program?
3. What other name is sometimes used for the keyboard?
4. What Python function is used to convert input values to integer?
5. What Python function is used to convert input values to float?

Expressions

In Python an **expression** is a combination of values, variables and operators that can be evaluated to produce a result. The values or variable used in an expression are known as **operands**.

The simplest expressions are those consisting only of values, for example

5 + 9

As you might expect, this evaluates to 14. If we simply type the expression in the Python Shell and press return, the expression will be evaluated and the result displayed on the screen, as shown below.

```
>>> 5 + 9
14
>>>
```

We can also build expressions using variables, for example

```
CostPerItem = 2.49
ItemsBought = 8

TotalCost = CostPerItem * ItemsBought

print("The total cost is: ", TotalCost)
```

If we run this program it will display

The total cost is: 19.92

Arithmetic operators

We refer to the addition sign (+) used in the above expressions as the **addition operator**. Python also makes use of several other **arithmetic operators**. In the following table assume that *a* and *b* are **integer variables** that have already been assigned the values 7 and 3 respectively.

Operator	Symbol	Example	Effect	Result
Addition	+	a + b	Adds the value stored in *a* to the value stored in *b*	10
Subtraction	−	a − b	Subtracts the value stored in *b* from the value stored in *a*	4
Multiplication	*	a * b	Multiplies the value stored in *a* by the value stored in *b*	21

| Division | / | a / b | Divides the value stored in **a** by the value stored in **b** | 2.3333 |
| **Exponential**[1] | ** | a ** b | Raises the value stored in **a** to the power of the value stored in **b** | 343 |

[1]Note: Some programming languages use the caret symbol (^) rather than the double asterisk as an exponential operator.

If either of the operands used in an arithmetic expression is of type float then the result will also be of type float. Note that there is a difference between 2 (an integer value) and 2.0 (a float value).

EXAM TIP

You can try out expressions simply by typing them in the Python Shell. You don't have to incorporate them into a program.

Complex expressions

Things become a bit more complicated when we have expressions that combine addition or subtraction with multiplication or division. For example, what would you expect the value of Result to be if we write the expression:
```
Result = 2 + 3 * 4?
```
You might expect the answer to be 20, but you'd be wrong – the correct answer is 14. This is because multiplication and division take priority over addition and subtraction, so we multiply 4 by 3, giving 12, then add 2 to the answer, giving 14. This is referred to as **priority of operators**.

We can change the order of evaluation by using brackets. If we write `Result = (2 + 3) * 4` then addition would be carried out first, followed by multiplication and the answer would be 20.

The rule for evaluating expressions is Brackets Off, Division and Multiplication, Addition and Subtraction (BODMAS).

EXAM TIP

Remember the BODMAS rule when evaluating expressions: Brackets Off, Division and Multiplication, Addition and Subtraction.

Quick Test 4

1. What would be the value of Result in the expression: Result = 23 / 4?
2. What would be the value of Result in the expression: Result = 2 ** 10?
3. What would be the value of Result in the expression: Result = 5 – 3 * 2?
4. What would be the value of Result in the expression: Result = 5 + 4 / 2?
5. What would be the value of Result in the expression: Result = (5 + 3) / 2?

Program control constructs

Any computer program can be written using only three basic control constructs, **sequence**, **iteration** (sometimes referred to as **repetition)** and **selection**.

The simplest construct is **sequence**. We've already seen an example of a program that consists simply of a sequence of instructions:

```
# assign values to variables

Surname = "McDonald"
Age = 16
Height = 62.5

# print values of variables

print(Surname)
print(Age)
print(Height)
```

As you can see, all the instructions in this program are simply executed one after the other. Execution starts at the beginning of the program and continues to the end.

Selection involves making choices. If a particular condition is true, then one set of instructions is executed, if it is untrue a different set of instructions is executed. Sometimes we may have to deal with compound conditions, where several choices have to be made before deciding which set of instructions to execute. We'll look at selection in more detail in the next section.

Iteration involves repeating sets of instructions. A set of instructions may be repeated a fixed number of times (count-controlled iteration) or until a specific condition occurs (condition-controlled iteration). In Python, **for loops** are used for count-controlled iteration and **while loops** for condition-controlled iteration. We'll look at iteration in more detail shortly.

EXAM TIP

Remember that any program can be constructed using only the sequence, iteration and selection constructs.

Sequence

Let's take a closer look at **sequence**, the simplest of our control constructs. Sequence can be represented graphically as follows:

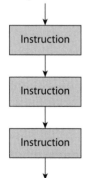

As you can see, a sequence consists of a series of instructions following one after the other. There is no decision-making, looping, or branching. Many simple programs, particularly those that are only designed to carry out a single task each time they are executed, consist of a sequence of instructions.

Imagine we have collected data about the highest temperature reached each day for a week and we want to input these values and calculate the average. We could write a short program as follows:

```
Temp1 = float (input ("enter temperature for day 1: "))
Temp2 = float (input ("enter temperature for day 2: "))
Temp3 = float (input ("enter temperature for day 3: "))
Temp4 = float (input ("enter temperature for day 4: "))
Temp5 = float (input ("enter temperature for day 5: "))
Temp6 = float (input ("enter temperature for day 6: "))
Temp7 = float (input ("enter temperature for day 7: "))

# calculate total and average temperatures

TotalTemp = Temp1 + Temp2 + Temp3 + Temp4 + Temp5 + Temp6 + Temp7

AvgTemp = TotalTemp / 7

# display average temperature

print ("The average temperature for the week was: ", AvgTemp)
```

```
>>> ================================ RESTART ================
================
>>>
enter temperature for day 1: 18.5
enter temperature for day 2: 16.3
enter temperature for day 3: 17.1
enter temperature for day 4: 19.2
enter temperature for day 5: 16.8
enter temperature for day 6: 18.7
enter temperature for day 7: 19.3
The average temperature for the week was: 17.985714285714284
>>>
```

EXAM TIP

The predefined function **round()** can be used to format output to the required number of decimal places.

The output from the program is shown alongside it. Note that the displayed temperature has lots of digits after the decimal point. If we want to keep this to two digits we can use the predefined function **round()** to format the output as follows:

```
print ("The average temperature for the week was:
", round (AvgTemp, 2))
```

We'll see shortly how the amount of repetition can be reduced by using the Iteration construct.

Quick Test 5

1. Which program control construct uses only a group of instructions executed one after the other?

2. Which program control construct involves repetition of instructions?

3. Which program control construct involves making choices?

4. Which type of loop is used in Python to repeat instructions a fixed number of times?

5. How would you display the contents of a variable named Result, correct to four decimal places?

Selection

We often find situations in programming where we only want to execute certain lines of code if a specified condition is true. We can do this by using an **if statement**.

Think about a machine selling tickets at a railway station. Passengers under the age of 16 are entitled to a discount, so the machine may ask for the passenger's age so that it can determine eligibility for a reduced fare. A simple program and its output are shown below:

```
# check age V1

Age = int(input("Please enter your age: "))

if Age < 16:

    print("You are eligible for a Junior Fare")
    print("Please insert £4")

else:

    print("You will need to pay the Full Fare")
    print("Please insert £8")
```

```
>>> ================================ RESTART ===============================
>>>
Please enter your age: 15
You are eligible for a Junior Fare
Please insert £4
>>> ================================ RESTART ===============================
>>>
Please enter your age: 18
You will need to pay the Full Fare
Please insert £8
```

Note the use of the **less than symbol (<)** to check if the **Age** entered is < 16. This is an example of a **comparison operator**. We'll examine these more closely in a moment. If the condition is **true**, one group of statements is executed. If it is **false**, another group of statements (following the else statement) is executed. The groups of statements are **indented** – this is how statements are grouped together in Python.

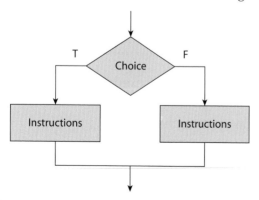

This diagram illustrates the operation of the simple selection process.

What if we want our program to show that users with an age greater than 59 are also entitled to a discount? We can amend it as shown below:

```
# check age V1

Age = int(input("Please enter your age: "))

if Age < 16:

    print("You are eligible for a Junior Fare")
    print("Please insert £4")

elif Age > 59:

    print("You are eligible for a Senior Fare")
    print("Please insert £4")

else:

    print("You will need to pay the Full Fare")
    print("Please insert £8")
```

```
>>> ============================ RESTART ============================
>>>
Please enter your age: 15
You are eligible for a Junior Fare
Please insert £4
>>> ============================ RESTART ============================
Please enter your age: 18
You will need to pay the Full Fare
Please insert £8
>>> ============================ RESTART ============================
>>>
Please enter your age: 62
You are eligible for a Senior Fare
Please insert £4
```

Note that we have added an **elif** clause. This is short for 'else if' and is effectively another **if statement** embedded within our original if statement. The diagram at the top of page 20 shows how this kind of **complex selection** process works.

Continues over page ⟶

Many programming languages have special-purpose statements, such as **case** or **switch**, for dealing with multiple conditions. Python does not have a special-purpose statement for doing this. If we need to test multiple conditions we can embed if statements to any depth we like. These are often known as **nested if statements**.

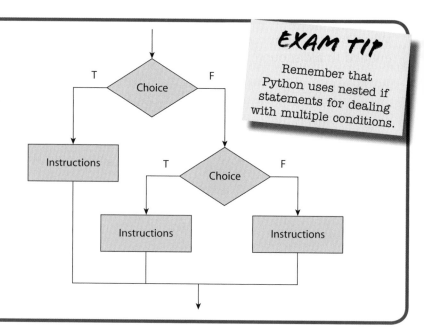

Comparison operators

We have already seen the **less than (<)** and **greater than (>) symbols** used as comparison operators. A number of other comparison operators can be used in Python. These are shown in the table below.

Operator	Function
<	less than
<=	less than or equal to
>	greater than
>=	greater than or equal to
==	equal to (equality)
!=	not equal to (inequality)

Some caution is required when using comparison operators. For example, we might say in English that 'passengers aged over 60 are entitled to a reduced fare' when what we really mean is 'passengers aged 60 or over are entitled to a reduced fare'. In our earlier example we used the statement:

```
if Age > 59
```

to express this. We could equally well write:

```
if Age >= 60
```

However, we could not write:

```
if Age > 60
```

as this would exclude passengers aged exactly 60.

We can also combine comparison operators using **and** and **or**. For example, we could do another version of our rail fares program:

```python
# check age V3

Age = int(input("Please enter your age: "))

if (Age < 16) or (Age > 59):

    print("You are eligible for a Reduced Fare")
    print("Please insert £4")

else:

    print("You will need to pay the Full Fare")
    print("Please insert £8")
```

```
>>> =============================== RESTART ===============================
>>>
Please enter your age: 15
You are eligible for a Reduced Fare
Please insert £4
>>> =============================== RESTART ===============================
>>>
Please enter your age: 25
You will need to pay the Full Fare
Please insert £8
>>> =============================== RESTART ===============================
>>>
Please enter your age: 61
You are eligible for a Reduced Fare
Please insert £4
```

Python also provides a **not** operator, which inverts the result of a logical comparison. For example, if the variable *Age* had a value of 59 then the comparison `Age >= 60` would give a result of False, but `not (Age >= 60)` would give a result of True.

Quick Test 6

1. What statement is used in Python for testing conditions?
2. What clause must be added to test for compound conditions?
3. How does Python handle multiple conditions?
4. What are the Python operators for equality and inequality?
5. How can comparison operators be combined in Python?

Iteration

When writing programs we often encounter situations where we have to repeat the same commands a number of times, as in the examples given earlier. The easiest way of dealing with these is to use **loops**. There are two types of loops:

- **Count-controlled loops** are used where the loop has to be executed a fixed number of times.
- **Condition-controlled loops** are used where the loop has to be executed until a particular condition occurs, for example where a specific value is input.

Count-controlled loops

Imagine that we want a program to display the first five entries in the 5 times table.

```
# 5 times table - version 1
tableno = 5
index = 0
print("The ", tableno, "times table")

index = index + 1
print(tableno," times ",  index, " = ", (tableno * index))

index = index + 1
print(tableno," times ",  index, " = ", (tableno * index))

index = index + 1
print(tableno," times ",  index, " = ", (tableno * index))

index = index + 1
print(tableno," times ",  index, " = ", (tableno * index))

index = index + 1
print(tableno," times ",  index, " = ", (tableno * index))
```

```
>>> ===================== RESTART =========================
=============================================================
>>>
The  5  times table
5  times  1  =  5
5  times  2  =  10
5  times  3  =  15
5  times  4  =  20
5  times  5  =  25
>>>
```

Again the program runs straight through from beginning to end but, as in the previous example on page 17, there is a lot of repetition of similar statements. We'll see in the next section how the amount of repetition can be reduced by using the iteration construct.

Let's try a different approach to our program for calculating the average temperature during a week. This is a fairly obvious situation for using a count-controlled loop, as we know that the main part of the program needs to be executed seven times, once for each day in the week.

Count-controlled loops in Python are known as **for loops**. The example below shows how we could write our program using a for loop. The output is shown alongside.

```python
# calculate average temperature over a week
# input data
TotalTemp = TotalTemp + Temp
for index in range (1, 8):
    print("Enter temperature for day ", index, ":", end= "")
    Temp = float(input())
    TotalTemp = TotalTemp + Temp
# calculate average temperature
AvgTemp = TotalTemp / 7
# display average temperature
print("The average temperature for the week was: ", AvgTemp)
```

```
Enter temperature for day  1 : 18.5
Enter temperature for day  2 : 16.3
Enter temperature for day  3 : 17.1
Enter temperature for day  4 : 19.2
Enter temperature for day  5 : 16.8
Enter temperature for day  6 : 18.7
Enter temperature for day  7 : 19.3
The average temperature for the week was: 17.985714285714284
```

Let's take a closer look at the loop itself.

```python
for index in range (1, 8):
print("Enter temperature for day ", index, ":", end= " ")
Temp = float(input())
TotalTemp = TotalTemp + Temp
```

The integer variable *index* is used as a **loop counter**, which takes each of the values used within the loop in turn. The numbers in brackets (1, 8) specify the initial and final values of the counter. You might be a bit surprised that the final value is 8 rather than 7, but the diagram below should make things clearer.

Before the loop begins the counter is set to the initial value. The indented lines show the instructions in the body of the loop. These are executed and then the value of the counter is incremented (increased) by 1. A check is then carried out to see whether the counter has reached its final value. If not, the body of the loop is executed again, otherwise the loop ends. In this example the loop ends when the counter reaches 8, after the body has been executed seven times.

EXAM TIP

A For Loop checks whether the terminating value has been exceeded at the end of the loop.

Let's look at another example – our 5 times table program, written using a for loop. The example on the next page shows the program and the output produced.

Initialise Counter → Instructions → Increment Counter → Counter = Limit? (F / T)

```
# 5 times table - version 2
tableno = 5
print("The ", tableno, "times table")
for index in range (1, tableno + 1):
    print(tableno," times ",  index, " = ", (tableno * index))
```

```
The  5  times table
5  times  1  =  5
5  times  2  =  10
5  times  3  =  15
5  times  4  =  20
```

This is certainly much clearer and simpler than the original version. Note that we need to specify the range of the loop as (1, 6) to make sure that the termination value is correct.

We can easily extend this program by allowing the user to specify the table to be printed, as shown below:

```
# any times table
tableno = int (input("Which table do you want to print? "))
print("The ", tableno, " times table")
for index in range (1, tableno + 1):
    print(tableno," times ", index, " = ", (tableno * index))
```

```
Which table do you want to print? 17
The  17  times table
17  times  1  =  17
17  times  2  =  34
17  times  3  =  51
17  times  4  =  68
17  times  5  =  85
```

(only the first five lines of output are shown)

Condition-controlled loops

For loops are great when we know exactly how many times we wish to execute the loop, but we often encounter situations where we do not know in advance how often the loop will need to be executed. To deal with this we need to use a different type of loop – a **condition-controlled loop** – which will stop executing when a particular condition is encountered, for example, if a specific value is entered by the user.

Condition-controlled loops are known in Python as **while loops**. Imagine we want to enter the height of each pupil in a class of unknown size and calculate the average height. The loop should terminate when we enter a zero (0). The program and output might look as shown below:

```python
# calculate average height of pupils in a class
Total = 0
Count = 0
Height = float(input("Enter height of first pupil: "))
while Height > 0 :
    Count = Count + 1
    Total = Total + Height
    Height = float(input("Enter height of next pupil; "))
if Count > 0:
    print("Number of pupils = ", Count)
    Average = Total / Count
    print("Average height = ", Average)
```

```
Enter height of first pupil: 62
Enter height of next  pupil: 64
Enter height of next  pupil: 69
Enter height of next  pupil: 68
Enter height of next  pupil: 66
Enter height of next  pupil: 65
Enter height of next  pupil: 67
Enter height of next  pupil: 68
Enter height of next  pupil: 65
Enter height of next  pupil: 66
Enter height of next  pupil: 0
Number of pupils = 10
Average height = 66.0
```

It is always possible to replace a for loop with an equivalent while loop which treats the number of times the loop is to be executed as the terminating condition. However, a while loop cannot generally be replaced by an equivalent for loop. A for loop is the preferred solution if a loop needs to be executed a fixed number of times.

Quick Test 7

1. Which type of Python loop is executed a fixed number of times?
2. Which type of Python loop tests the exit condition at the beginning of the loop?
3. Which type of Python loop tests the exit condition at the end of the loop?
4. If you want the counter for a Python loop to go through the numbers 1 to 10, what initial and final values should be specified?
5. A while loop can always be replaced by an equivalent for loop – true or false?

Predefined functions

A **function** is a piece of code used in a larger program to carry out a specific task. The advantages of using functions include:

- reducing duplication of code
- breaking complex problems down into simpler pieces
- making programs more readable.

There are two basic types of functions; **predefined functions** (also known as built-in functions) and **user-defined functions**. In this course we only consider predefined functions. We have already encountered several predefined functions, including **input()**, **print()**, **int()** and **float()**. Let's review them briefly.

The **input()** function is used to get information from the keyboard and the **print()** function is used to display output on the screen, as seen in the following example program:

```
# input and print functions

Name = input("Please enter your forename: ")

Height = input("Please enter your height in inches: ")

print("Hello ", Name, " - you are ", Height, "inches tall")
```

```
Please enter your forename: Jack
Please enter your height in inches: 68
Hello  Jack  - you are 68 inches tall
```

The result returned by the **input()** function is always of type **string**. This is OK in the example given above, but what if we wanted to do some arithmetic on *Height:* for example convert it to centimetres? We would need to convert the string variable to a float variable before we can carry out the arithmetic. This can be done using the **float()** function as shown below:

```
# input and print functions V2

Name = input("Please enter your forename: ")

Height = input("Please enter your height in inches: ")

print("Hello ", Name, " - you are ", Height, "inches tall")

print("This is equivalent to", float(Height) * 2.54, "centimetres")
```

```
Please enter your forename: Jack
Please enter your height in inches: 68
Hello  Jack  - you are 68 inches tall
This is equivalent to 172.72 centimetres
```

We can also use the **int()** function to convert a string or float value to an integer.

Predefined mathematical functions

Several common mathematical functions are available as predefined functions in Python. The simplest is **abs**, which returns the absolute value of a number, i.e. the unsigned value. The number returned by abs is of the same type as the number passed to it. For example:

```python
print(abs(-4.2))
```

would print 4.2.

The function **min** returns the smallest value in a list of values. For example:

```python
print min(5, 7, 2, 3, 9, 6)
```

would print the value 2.

Similarly, the function **max** returns the largest value in a list of values. For example:

```python
print max(5, 7, 2, 3, 9, 6)
```

would print the value 9.

> **EXAM TIP**
>
> The **sum()** function is a useful way of adding up a sequence of numbers in Python.

The **round** function rounds a float value to a specified number of digits. You must specify the number to be rounded and the number of decimal places you want to display. For example:

```python
print(round(1.2325, 2))
```

would print 1.23

Lastly, the **sum** function adds numbers in a sequence. By using range (which we introduced along with the **for** statement) you can calculate the sum of the first 10 positive integers:

```python
print(sum(range(1, 10)))
```

would print the value 55.

Python offers a number of additional mathematical functions, including trig and logarithmic functions, via the **math module**, which can be made available to your programs by inserting the line:

```python
import math
```

near the beginning of the program. The math module also provides values for the constants *pi* and *e*.

Quick Test 8

1. Which function is used to add a sequence of numbers?
2. What type of data does the input() function return?
3. What module needs to be loaded to use trigonometric functions in Python?
4. What unit must angles be expressed in to use them in Python functions?
5. Which constants does Python supply values for?

Low-level operations and structure

Binary representation

It is important to remember that although we may work with familiar concepts such as **integers**, **floating-point numbers** and **strings**, everything inside the computer is stored in **binary** format and consists only of 0s and 1s.

Integers (whole numbers) are fairly straightforward. An integer is usually stored as a fixed-length binary number. The range of positive integers that can be represented by X binary digits is 2^x (2 to the power x). This range starts at 0, so the range that can be represented will always be 0 to $2^x - 1$. For example, 16 bits are required to represent unsigned integers in the range 0 to 65535. The highest value would consist only of 1s, as shown below.

1	1	1	1	1	1	1	1	1	1	1	1	1	1	1	1

Signed integers can be represented by using one of the bits to represent the sign.

You may have seen very large or very small numbers written as a number between 1 and 10 multiplied by a power of 10. This is a notation known as **standard form** or **scientific form**. For example:

$4.56 \times 10^3 = 4.56 \times 1000 = 4560$
$6.78 \times 10^{-2} = 6.78 \times 0.01 = 0.0678$

Floating-point numbers (real numbers) are stored in a computer using a similar principle, but instead of using a power of 10 they are stored using a power of 2. The decimal part of the number is known as the **mantissa**, and the power of 2 to which it is raised is known as the **exponent**. A floating-point number is represented by $M \times 2^E$, where the **mantissa (M)** is a binary fraction starting with a 1 and the **exponent (E)** is a binary integer.

The mantissa determines the degree of **accuracy** or **precision** with which numbers can be represented, while the exponent determines the **range of numbers** that can be represented. So, increasing the number of bits assigned to the mantissa will increase the accuracy with which the number can be represented, at the expense of decreasing the range of numbers that can be represented.

This example shows how 6.6 could be represented using 16 bits, 10 bits for the mantissa and 6 bits for the exponent, but in reality at least 32 bits would be used:

EXAM TIP

The mantissa determines the degree of **accuracy or precision** with which floating-point numbers can be represented, while the exponent determines the **range of numbers** that can be represented.

Mantissa										Exponent					
0	1	1	0	1	0	0	0	0	0	0	0	0	0	1	1

Characters, such as letters, digits and symbols, are also stored in binary form. Each character is usually stored in one byte (8 bits). The group of characters used by a computer system is known as the **character set**. Each character in the set is assigned a number, which can be converted to binary. This was originally done using the **American Standard Code for Information Interchange (ASCII)**, a 7-bit code that can represent 128 (2^7) different characters. Extended ASCII uses all 8 bits allowing the representation of 256 different characters.

ASCII does not allow the representation of foreign language characters. **Unicode**, which was developed to overcome this limitation, uses 16 bits, allowing the representation of 65,536 different characters. This lets it represent characters in languages like Greek or Arabic, but it requires twice as much storage space as ASCII.

Bit-mapped images, such as those produced by a drawing program, are stored as an array of **pixels**. Each pixel has a binary value corresponding to a colour. In the simplest case we could use only 1 bit to represent each pixel – it could be 0 for black and 1 for white. If we used 8 bits we could represent 256 (2^8) different colours.

The number of bits used to store the colour of each pixel is known as the **bit depth**. The number of pixels in a given area is known as the **resolution**. High resolution images are of better quality, but they occupy more space. They are often compressed to reduce the storage space required and make them quicker to download.

Vector images, such as those produced by a drawing program, store images as a collection of shapes or objects, each with its own properties. For example, the properties of a square might include x and y coordinates, width, height, line colour, thickness, fill colour and style. Vector images generally occupy less storage space than bit-mapped images. They are resolution-independent, so they can be resized without loss of quality, unlike bit-mapped images, which can look blocky or pixelated when enlarged.

Program instructions (machine code) are also stored internally in binary format. For example an ADD instruction may have the format: **ADD R1, R2, R3** meaning 'add the contents of Register R1 to the contents of R2 and store the result in R3'. The instruction itself is often referred to as the **operation code** or **opcode** and the data it works on are called **operands**.

	Opcode				Operand 1				Operand 2				Operand 3			
Assembly language	ADD				R1				R2				R3			
Machine code	1	0	1	0	0	0	0	1	0	0	1	0	0	0	1	1

Quick Test 9

1. What range of unsigned integers can be stored as a 16-bit binary number?
2. What determines the degree of accuracy of a floating-point number represented in binary?
3. Why has Unicode superseded ASCII as the preferred method of representing characters?
4. How many colours can be represented in a bit-mapped image using 8 bits per pixel?

Computer architecture

All computer systems have the same major components. These components and the relationships between them are shown in the diagram below.

- **Central processing unit (CPU)** or processor, which executes programs.
- **Primary storage** or main memory, which holds the programs currently being executed and the data they are processing.
- **Secondary storage** or backing storage, for example hard disks or flash drives, which store programs and data.
- **Input devices**, such as keyboards and mice.
- **Output devices**, such as display screens or printers.

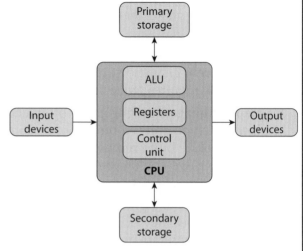

Many of the processors used in tablets and smartphones are designed by a British company, ARM. Modern computing devices often use **multiple-core processors**, allowing several tasks to be carried out simultaneously.

CPU components

A CPU has three major internal components.

- The **arithmetic and logic unit (ALU)** executes the program instructions, carrying out calculations, boolean operations (AND, OR, NOT) and comparisons.
- The **registers** are small areas of very fast memory, used while instructions are being executed. They hold the instructions currently being executed, data being transferred to/from memory and the addresses of the memory locations being accessed by the CPU.
- The **control unit** coordinates the operations of the other components and ensures that everything takes place in the correct sequence. It sends out control signals to move data between registers, read or write memory and control the input and output devices.

EXAM TIP

Remember that the CPU has three main components: the arithmetic and logic unit (ALU), the registers and the control unit.

Processor busses

The processor busses are groups of wires connecting the CPU to the main memory.

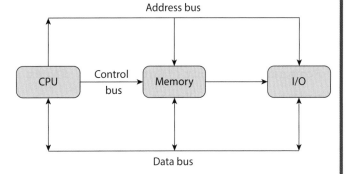

- The **data bus** transfers data between the CPU and the memory. Its width, determined by the number of lines used, is an important factor in system performance. Each line can carry 1 bit, so a 32-bit data bus can transfer 32 bits simultaneously.

- The **address bus** specifies the memory addresses being accessed. The width of the address bus determines the number of memory locations the CPU can access. A 32-bit address bus can access up to 2^{32} memory locations.

- The **control bus** carries control signals. A read signal tells the memory to put data at the address specified by the address bus on to the data bus. A write signal tells the memory to take the data on the data bus and put it in the location specified by the address bus.

EXAM TIP

The width of busses is important. A wide data bus improves system performance while a wider address bus allows more memory to be addressed.

Interfaces

The CPU is connected to the I/O devices and the backing storage by **interfaces**, responsible for buffering, data format conversion, voltage conversion, protocol conversion and the handling of status signals. Common interfaces include **VGA** (video graphics array) and **HDMI** (high definition multimedia interface), both used for connecting monitors, and **USB** (universal serial bus), used for connecting a range of devices, including mice, printers and webcams.

Quick Test 10

1. What is the name given to the groups of wires connecting the CPU to the main memory?
2. Which group of wires is responsible for starting read and write operations?
3. What is an HDMI interface used for?
4. Which type of interface is a printer normally connected to?

Using programming constructs

As we have already seen, any computer program can be written using only three basic constructs – sequence, iteration, and selection. Let's look at these again briefly:

Sequence simply means that program statements are normally executed one after another, reading from top to bottom.

```
Forename = input("Enter your first name: ")
print("Hello", Forename)
```

Iteration (sometimes called **repetition**) means that a group of program statements is executed repeatedly. This can either be done a fixed number of times, or until certain conditions occur, such as inputting a value indicating the end of the data.

```
Total = 0
for index in range (1, 4):
    print("Enter an integer: ", end= "")
    Number = float(input())
    Total = Total + Number
print("The total of the integers entered
is: ", int(Total))
```

Selection means that a choice has to be made between different routes through the program, usually depending on the value of the input data. For example, we might want to follow different paths if the input data referred to people of different ages.

```
Age = int(input("Please enter your
age: "))
if Age < 16:
    print("Sorry, you are under age")
else:
    print("Please go ahead")
```

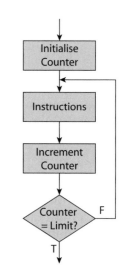

Pseudocode

It is common practice to design programs using a **program design language**, often referred to as **Pseudocode.** The basic principle is that it should lie somewhere between standard English and a programming language. The big advantage in using Pseudocode is that it can easily be translated into any programming language – it is not tied to a specific language.

Let's look briefly at how we could represent our basic programming constructs in Pseudocode. We'll write Pseudocode keywords in capitals to distinguish them from our program code.

Sequences usually consist of simple programming language statements like assignments, input/output statements and calculations.

Assignments can be represented by **SET ... TO ...**, for example:

Pseudocode	Python
SET count TO 1	count = 1

Input is usually written using **RECEIVE ... FROM ...**, for example:

Pseudocode	Python
RECEIVE input_value FROM KEYBOARD	input_value = input()

Output is normally written as **SEND ... TO ...**, for example:

Pseudocode	Python
SEND output_value TO DISPLAY	print (output_value)

Note that two Pseudocode statements are required to represent a simple Python input statement containing a prompt:

Pseudocode	Python
SEND "Enter T or F: " TO DISPLAY RECEIVE reply FROM KEYBOARD	reply = input ("Enter T or F: ")

Continues over page ⟶

Calculations are normally written using the standard programming notation for mathematical symbols, for example: + (add), − (subtract), * (multiply), / (divide), etc.

Comparisons are also written using standard mathematical symbols such as =, ≠, >, <, >=, <=, etc. Note that the symbol used for **not equal to** (≠) is different from the one used in Python (!=).

Pseudocode	Python
SET sum TO num1 + num2	`sum = num1 + num2`

Condition-controlled iteration is usually written as **WHILE ... DO ... END WHILE**, for example:

Pseudocode	Python

WHILE input_value > 0 DO
  SET total TO total + input_value
END WHILE
	`while (input_value > 0) :`
	`    total = total + 1`

Count-controlled iteration is normally written as **FOR ... FROM ... TO ... DO ... END FOR**, for example:

Pseudocode	Python
FOR count FROM 1 TO 20 SEND count TO DISPLAY END FOR	`for count in range(1, 21) :` `    print (count)`

Selection is usually written as **IF ... THEN ... (ELSE) ... END IF**, for example:

Pseudocode	Python

IF age >= 65 THEN
  SET pensioners TO pensioners + 1
ELSE
  SET others TO others + 1
END IF
	`if age >= 65 :`
	`    pensioners = pensioners + 1`
	`else:`
	`    others = others + 1`

A **complex selection** could be written as:

Pseudocode	Python

IF age >= 65 THEN
    SET pensioners TO pensioners + 1
ELSE IF age >= 16 THEN
    SET juveniles TO juveniles + 1
ELSE
    SET others TO others + 1
END IF
	```if age >= 65 :```
	``` pensioners = pensioners + 1```
	```elif age <= 16:```
	``` juveniles = juveniles + 1```
	```else:```
	``` others = others + 1```

EXAM TIP

In Pseudocode we use explicit END WHILE and END FOR statements to indicate the end of While and For Loops. In Python these are unnecessary as the end of the indented code indicates the end of the loop.

Quick Test 11

1. What would be the Python equivalent of the following fragment of Pseudocode?

    FOR index FROM 1 TO 10

    　SEND index TO DISPLAY

    END FOR

2. Why are explicit **END WHILE** and **END FOR** statements unnecessary in Python?

3. How could the following Python code fragment be expressed in Pseudocode?

    ```
    response = input("Enter Y or N: ")
    ```

    ```
    while (response != "Y") and (response != "N"):
    ```

    ```
    response = input("You must enter Y or N: ")
    ```

4. What Python statement is used to handle compound conditions?

5. What single Python statement would be equivalent to the following fragment of Pseudocode?

    SEND "Enter Y or N: " TO DISPLAY

    RECEIVE response FROM KEYBOARD

Using programming constructs: an example

We have already looked at simple programs that use each of our programming constructs separately. Let's look now at a slightly more complex example where we use three constructs. Consider the following scenario:

A secondary class is made of a mixture of male and female pupils. We want to write a program to calculate the average heights of the male and female pupils separately, as well as the average height for the whole class. The number of pupils in the class is not known at the start of the program. The program should terminate when an age of zero or less is entered.

We'll design our program using Pseudocode. Let's start by declaring and initialising some variables to hold our counts and totals.	SET female_count TO 0 SET female_total TO 0 SET male_count TO 0 SET male_total TO 0 SET all_count TO 0 SET all_total TO 0
Now we want to read the height of the first pupil.	SEND "Enter Height in centimetres:" TO DISPLAY RECEIVE height FROM KEYBOARD
Next we need a while loop that will repeat until a value of zero is entered for **height**. The first thing we want to do within this loop is to input the **gender** of the pupil.	WHILE height > 0 DO SEND "Enter Gender (M/F): " TO DISPLAY RECEIVE gender FROM KEYBOARD

Now we'll use another while loop that will keep repeating until a correct value of "M" or "F" is entered.	WHILE (gender ≠ "M") AND (gender ≠ "F") DO
	SEND "Gender must be M or F" TO DISPLAY
	SEND "Enter Gender (M/F): " TO DISPLAY
	RECEIVE gender FROM KEYBOARD
	END WHILE

> **EXAM TIP**
>
> It is always a good idea to explicitly set any newly-declared variable that will be used as a counter to zero. Some programming languages do this automatically but others do not, so explicit setting is the safest approach.

If the user entered "M" then the condition (**gender ≠ "F"**) would be **True**. However, if they entered "F" then the condition (**gender ≠ "M"**) would be **True**. Thus the compound condition would always be **True**, irrespective of the value entered and the loop would repeat indefinitely.

The condition **WHILE (gender ≠ "M") AND (gender ≠ "F") DO** is **False** if either "M" or "F" is entered, so the loop will terminate as expected. Always be careful when using **AND** or **OR** in compound conditions. The usage often seems contrary to what you would expect from everyday English.

EXAM TIP

Take a good look at the format of the compound conditional statement: **WHILE (gender ≠ "M") AND (gender ≠"F") DO.** We're expecting the user to enter "M" **OR** "F", so why don't we write: **WHILE (gender ≠ "M") OR (gender ≠"F") DO?**

Now that we have entered the height of the pupil and validated the gender, we can continue with our remaining calculations, incrementing our counters and adding the height to the appropriate total. This is fairly straightforward.	**IF gender = "M" THEN**
	
	  SET male_total TO male_total + height
	
	  SET male_count = TO male_count + 1
	ELSE IF gender = "F" THEN
	
	  SET female_total TO female_total + height
	
	  SET female_count TO female_count + 1
	END IF

After this we want to print a blank line for formatting purposes, read the height of the next pupil, terminate our while loop and print another blank line.	**SEND "" TO DISPLAY**
	
	  SEND "Enter Height in centimetres: "
	  TO DISPLAY
	
	  RECEIVE height FROM KEYBOARD
	END WHILE
	
	  SEND "" TO DISPLAY

We have now collected all our data and we want to process it. First we'll check to see if there were any female pupils and, if so, calculate and print their average height.	**IF (female_count ≠ 0) THEN**
	
	  SET female_average TO female_total / female_count
	
	  SEND "The average height for female pupils is"
	  TO DISPLAY
	
	  SEND female_average TO DISPLAY
	END IF

Next we'll check to see if there were any male pupils and, if so, calculate and print their average height.	**IF (male_count ≠ 0) THEN**
	  SET male_average TO male_total / male_count
	
	  SEND "The average height for male pupils is" TO
	  DISPLAY
	
	  SEND female_average TO DISPLAY
	END IF

Continues over page ⟶

Finally, if either or both female and male pupils were present we can calculate the total and average heights for all pupils and print the average. If neither males nor females were present we can print a message saying that "No data was entered".	**IF (female_count ≠ 0) OR (male_count ≠ 0) THEN**
	  SET all_count TO female_count + male_count
	  SET all_total TO female_total + male_total
	  SET all_average TO all_total / all_count
	  SEND "The average height for all pupils is" TO DISPLAY
	  SEND all_average TO DISPLAY
	ELSE
	  SEND "No data was entered" TO DISPLAY
	END IF

Once we have designed our program using Pseudocode we can write it in Python. The complete program is shown below:

```
1   # Program 2.1 Calculate separate average heights
2   # for male and female pupils and for whole class.
3
4   female_count = 0
5   female_total = 0
6   male_count = 0
7   male_total = 0
8   all_count = 0
9   all_total = 0
10
11  # Read height of first pupil
12
13  height = float(input("Enter Height in centimetres: "))
14
15  while height > 0:
16      gender = input("Enter Gender (M/F): ")
17
18  # Validate gender
19
20      while (gender != "M") and (gender != "F"):
21          print("Gender must be M or F")
22          gender = input("Enter Gender (M/F): ")
23
24  # End validation loop
25
26      if gender == "M":
27          male_total = male_total + height
28          male_count = male_count + 1
29
```

```
30      elif gender == "F":
31          female_total = female_total + height
32          female_count = female_count + 1
33
34   # Print a blank line and read height of next pupil
35
36      print("")
37      height = float(input("Enter height in centimetres: "))
38
39   # End of while loop
40
41   print("")
42
43   if (female_count != 0):
44       female_average = female_total / female_count
45       print("The average height for female pupils is", female_average)
46
47   if (male_count != 0):
48       male_average = male_total / male_count
49       print("The average height for male pupils is", male_average)
50
51   if (female_count != 0) or (male_count != 0):
52       all_count = female_count + male_count
53       all_total = female_total + male_total
54       all_average = all_total / all_count
55       print("The average height for all pupils is", all_average)
56
57   else:
58       print("No data was entered")
```

Quick Test 12

1. A user has been asked to enter "Y" or "N". Write a Python code fragment to check whether the data entered is correct and, if not, ask for it to be entered again.

2. A program is required to ask 10 users to enter their gender (M or F), height (cm) and weight (kg). It should keep count of the number of males (mcount) with a height greater than 180 cm and weight greater than 60 kg and the number of females (fcount) with a height greater than 160 cm and weight greater than 50 kg. Write a suitable program in Python. There is no need to validate the gender.

Simple data types: integer

Python has three numeric data types: **integers**, **floating point numbers** and **complex numbers**. We'll look at the first two in more detail. Complex numbers are outwith the scope of this course.

All the numeric data types share several features. The standard arithmetic operators (+, −, *, /, //, % and **) are all available for all the numeric types, and all can be compared using the comparison operators that we looked at earlier. Numbers can be converted from one type to another.

Python provides several more advanced mathematical functions, including **abs(x)** and **pow(x, y)** and others are available via the **math module**.

Integers

Integers are whole numbers, for example 2, 5, 7, 42, 64, 512, 1024, etc. They have no decimal part and can be either positive or negative. In Python, integers can be of any size. The Python data type for integers is **int**.

Let's have a look at a short program that demonstrates the features of Python integers.

```python
 1  # Program 2.2: Integers
 2
 3  # Read Integers
 4
 5  int1 = int(input("Enter first integer: "))
 6  int2 = int(input("Enter second integer: "))
 7  print("")
 8
 9  # Display Integers
10
11  print("The first integer (int1) is: ", int1)
12  print("The second integer (int2) is: ", int2)
13  print("")
14
15  # Integer Operations
16
17  print("Addition: int1 + int2 = ", int1 + int2)
18  print("Subtraction: int1 - int2 = ", int1 - int2)
19  print("Multiplication: int1 * int2 = ", int1 * int2)
20  print("Exponentiation: int1 ** int2 = ", int1 ** int2)
21  print("Division: int1 / int2 = ", int1 / int2)
22  print("Integer Division: int1 // int2 = ", int1 // int2)
23  print("")
24
```

```
25 | # Convert to Float
26 |
27 | float1 = float(int1)
28 | float2 = float(int2)
29 |
30 | print("The first float (float1) is: ", float1)
31 | print("The second float (float2) is: ", float2)
```

The output from this program would be as follows:

```
Enter first integer: 5
Enter second integer: 5

The first integer (int1)is:  5
The second integer (int2) is:  5

Addition: int1 + int2 =  10
Subtraction: int1 - int2 =  0
Multiplication: int1 * int2 =  25
Exponentiation: int1 ** int2 =  3125
Division: int1 / int2 =  1.0
Integer Division: int1 // int2 =  1

The first float (float1)is:  5.0
The second float (float2) is:  5.0
```

EXAM TIP

Integers are used for storing **counted** values. One common use is as a counter in for loops.

Integers can be input from the keyboard using the **input()** function (lines 5 and 6). By default the **input()** function returns a string value, so if we want to ensure that our input is stored as an integer we must also use the **int()** function.

Integers can be displayed on the screen using the **print()** function (lines 11 and 12).

Various arithmetic operations can be carried out on integers (lines 17–22). Take particular note of lines 21–22 and the associated output. If we divide one integer by another using the / operator the result will be a float value. Python will convert it automatically and display it correctly. If we wish to produce an integer value we need to use the **integer division operator (//)**. This will simply strip off any fractional part in the result – it will not round.

We can explicitly convert integer values to float values by using the **float()** function (lines 30–31).

Continues over page ⟶

Simple data types: float

Floating point

Floating point numbers are those that have a decimal part, for example, 2.1, 3.14159265, 98.6, 131.0, etc. Floating point numbers are often referred to as **real numbers** and can be either positive or negative. The Python data type for floating point numbers is **float**. Python floating point numbers can be of any size.

Let's have a look at a short program that demonstrates the features of Python floating point numbers:

```
 1   # Program 2.3: Floating Point
 2
 3   # Read floats
 4
 5   float1 = float(input("Enter first float: "))
 6   float2 = float(input("Enter second float: "))
 7   print("")
 8
 9   # Display floats
10
11   print("The first float (float1) is: ", float1)
12   print("The second float (float2) is: ", float2)
13   print("")
14
15   # Float Operations
16
17   print("Addition: float1 + float2 = ", "%0.2f" % (float1 + float2))
18   print("Subtraction: float1 - float2 = ", "%0.2f" % (float1 - float2))
19   print("Multiplication: float1 * float2 = ", "%0.2f" % (float1 * float2))
20   print("Exponentiation: float1 ** float2 = ", "%0.2f" % (float1 ** float2))
21   print("Division: float1 / float2 = ", "%0.2f" % (float1 / float2))
22   print("")
23
24   # Convert to Integer
25
26   int1 = int(float1)
27   int2 = int(float2)
28
29   print("The first integer (int1) is: ", int1)
30   print("The second integer (int2) is: ", int2)
```

The output from this program would be as follows:

```
Enter first float: 5.3
Enter second float: 2.1

The first float (float1) is:   5.3
The second float (float2) is:   2.1

Addition: float1 + float2 = 7.40
Subtraction: float1 - float2 = 3.20
Multiplication: float1 * float2 = 11.13
Exponentiation: float1 ** float2 = 33.19
Division: float1 / float2 = 2.52

The first integer (int1) is:   5
The second integer (int2) is:   2
```

Floating point numbers can be input from the keyboard using the **input()** function (lines 5 and 6). By default the **input()** function returns a string value, so if we wish to ensure that our input is stored as a floating point number we must also use the **float()** function.

Floating point numbers can be displayed on the screen using the **print()** function (lines 11 and 12).

Various arithmetic operations can be carried out on floating point numbers (lines 17–21). Python normally displays floating point numbers using the full number of decimal places stored internally. This can look untidy on output, so we often want to restrict the number of decimal places displayed. There are various ways of doing this – one of the easiest is to precede the value to be displayed by a format specifier such as "%0.2f", as shown on lines 17–21.

We can explicitly convert float values to integer by using the **int()** function (lines 29–30). The **int()** function always rounds down.

> **EXAM TIP**
>
> Floating point numbers are used for storing measured values, such as weights, lengths, distances, etc.

Quick Test 13

1. What kind of variable would you use to store the number of cars seen travelling from Glasgow to Edinburgh on a Monday morning?

2. What type of variable would you use to store the distance travelled by a car going from Glasgow to Edinburgh?

3. What kind of variable would you use as a loop counter?

4. What type of variable would you use to store the average height of all the students in a class?

Simple data types: string and boolean

String

In Python a string is simply a sequence of characters, such as letters, digits or symbols. We can assign a value to a string variable using the normal = operator. The value to be assigned is enclosed in quotes, for example:

```
day = "Monday"
```

Python provides a number of **string functions** that can be used to manipulate strings. The following program shows how some of them are used:

```
 1  today = 'Monday'
 2  time = 'Morning'
 3
 4  # the len() function can be used to find out the length of a string
 5
 6  print(len(today))
 7  print(len(time))
 8
 9  # we can extract one or more characters from a string
10  # note that the characters are enclosed in square
11  # brackets and are numbered starting from 0
12
13  print(today[0])
14  print(today[0:3])
15
16  # we can join or concatenate strings using the + operator
17
18  print(today + ' ' + time)
```

Running the program produces the following output:

```
6
7
M
Mon
Monday Morning
```

Boolean

Boolean variables, often referred to simply as **booleans**, can only take the values **True** or **False**. These values are always written with a capital letter. The main use of booleans is in comparison statements – the result of a comparison is always a boolean value, as shown in the adjacent code fragment and the associated output.

```
1  x = 10          False
2  y = 12          False
3                  True
4  print(x == y)
5  print(x > y)
6  print(x < y)
```

Although you will rarely see boolean variables used directly in a program, they are used indirectly every time you evaluate a comparison, for example in an if statement or a while loop, as shown below.

Code	Meaning
if (age > 64)	if the expression (age > 64) is True
while (x != 0)	while the expression (x = 0) is False

Rule	Expression	Evaluates to
If any part of a compound expression using **and** is False, the whole expression is False.	True and True	True
	True and False	False
	False and True	False
	False and False	False
If any part of a compound expression using **or** is True, the whole expression is True.	True and True	True
	True and False	True
	False and True	True
	False and False	False
Not False is the same as True and not True is the same as False.	not False	True
	not True	False

Quick Test 14

1. What would be the output from the following program fragment?

    ```
    a = 5
    b = 9
    print((a == 5) and (b == 9))
    ```

2. What would be the output from the following program fragment?

    ```
    a = 5
    b = 9
    print((a == 9) or (b == 5))
    ```

3. How could you extract the word "Hello" from the phrase "Hello World"?

4. How could you print the length of the phrase "Hello World"?

Testing digital solutions

Errors

Programming is a complex process and it is easy for errors to occur. It is therefore necessary to **test computer programs thoroughly** to ensure that they work correctly under all circumstances. Errors in programs are often referred to as **bugs**, supposedly because early computers, which made use of electrical relays, suffered problems due to insects (bugs) shorting these relays. The process of testing programs is sometimes referred to as **debugging**.

Three different types of errors are commonly found in programs: syntax errors, run-time errors and logic errors.

Syntax errors

Syntax errors are errors in the structure or grammar of the program. They are fairly easy to find as they are generally detected by the compiler or interpreter when attempting to convert the source program to machine code. The following code fragment has two syntax errors: a quote character ('') has been omitted in line 4 and there is a bracket missing from the end of line 7.

```
1  # Program 2.4: Syntax Errors
2
3  number1 = float(input("Enter the first number: "))
4  number2 = float(input("Enter the second number: ))
5  print("")
6
7  print("number1 plus number2 = ", number1 + number2
8  print("number1 divided by number2 = ", number1 / number2)
```

If we attempt to run this program we will get an error message and a visual indicator (a red bar) showing where the error occurs. (EOL means 'End of Line'.)

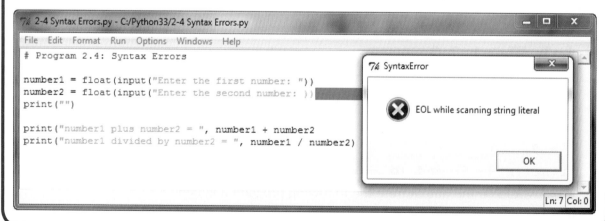

If we correct this and try to run the program again, we will get a further error:

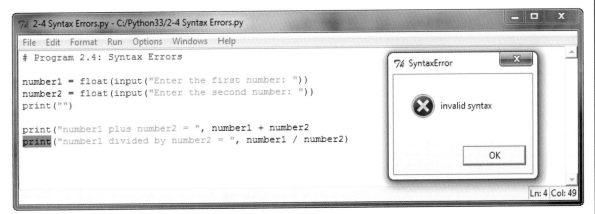

Note that this time the error indicator appears on the line following the error. This is fairly common as the interpreter only realises that an error has occurred when it reaches the start of the next line. The error message is not particularly informative – this is also fairly common. Once we correct this error the program will run successfully.

Run-time errors

Run-time errors occur when something goes wrong during the execution of a seemingly-correct program. One of the most common run-time errors is an attempt to divide by zero. If we run the same program, entering a value of 0 for the second number, the program will run correctly until it attempts to divide by zero and will then fail. The output will be as follows:

```
Enter the first number: 23
Enter the second number: 0

number1 plus number2 =   23.0
Traceback (most recent call last):
  File "c:/Python33/2-4 Syntax Errors.py", line 8, in <module>
    print("number1 divided by number2 = ", number1 / number2)
ZeroDivisionError: float division by zero
```

Continues over page ⟶

This can be averted by amending the program code to ensure that division by zero is never attempted:

```
1   # Program 2.5: Avoid Division by Zero
2
3   number1 = float(input("Enter the first number: "))
4   number2 = float(input("Enter the second number: "))
5   print("")
6
7   print("number1 plus number2 = ", number1 + number2)
8   if number2 != 0:
9       print("number1 divided by number2 = ", number1 / number2)
10  else:
11      print("division by zero is not allowed")
```

Any time you use division in a program you should insert a check to ensure that you are not trying to divide by zero.

Logic errors

Logic errors occur when a syntactically-correct program runs successfully but produces an unexpected result. For example, if we have a situation where those aged under 16 or over 64 are admitted to a museum free of charge and we wish to write a program to check eligibility, the programmer might code this as follows:

```
1   #Program 2.6: Logic Error
2
3   age = int(input("Please enter your age: "))
4
5   if ((age < 16) and (age > 64)):
6       print("You are entitled to free admission")
7   else:
8       print("You are not entitled to free admission")
```

When this is run it will always produce the following output, no matter what age is entered:

```
You are not entitled to free admission
```

There is a fault in line 5 of the program. It is impossible for age to be < 16 **and** > 64. If this line is corrected to read: **if ((age< 16) or (age> 64)):** the program will now run correctly.

If you need to use compound comparison statements you should always test them carefully to ensure that they function as expected.

Another common type of logic error is the **infinite loop**, a sequence of instructions in a computer program which loops endlessly. This is usually because the loop has no terminating condition or a terminating condition that can never be met.

The following program will never terminate because no attempt is ever made to change the value of x, so it will always remain as 1.

```
x = 1
while(x == 1):
        print("Infinite Loop")
```

The next example is a bit more complex. This program will never terminate because representation of floating point numbers is inexact, so the terminating condition (x = 1) will never be met.

```
x = 0.1
while x != 1:
        print(x)
        x =   x + 0.1
```

Since tests for equality or inequality are prone to failure it is safer to use greater-than or less-than tests when dealing with floating-point values. For example, instead of checking whether x == 1.1, we could check whether (x <= 1.0) or (x < 1.1). Either of these would be certain to exit eventually.

Quick Test 15

1. What type of error can be caused by a missing bracket?
2. What type of error results from attempting to divide by zero?
3. What type of error occurs as a result of incorrect comparisons?
4. When is a syntax error normally discovered?
5. How do we know that a logic error has occurred?

Finding and fixing errors

The process of running a program with the intention of finding and fixing errors is usually referred to as **testing** and should be carried out systematically, according to a predetermined plan. The programs we have seen to date have functioned as complete, stand-alone programs. In practice, most programs are made up of a series of modules or subprograms, which are written and tested independently and then assembled to produce a complete program. The information given in this section about the testing of programs is equally applicable to the testing of subprograms.

Choosing test data

There are three main categories of test data:

- **Normal data** is the type of data that the program is likely to encounter during a typical run. The program should be able to deal easily with this.
- **Extreme data** is data at the boundaries of the program's capabilities. The program should still be able to cope with this, but it may require more care on the part of the programmer.
- **Exceptional data** is incorrect and should not be processed by the program. However, the program should still be able to detect and reject it in order to avoid incorrect output or program crashes.

Imagine that you are writing a program to calculate the average temperature over 7 days. The program should handle temperatures in the range −20°C to 60°C. The program could look as follows:

> **EXAM TIP**
>
> Avoid the temptation to use 'real-world' data as test data. It does not normally contain enough extreme or exceptional cases to test a program effectively.

```
1  #Program 2.7 Test Data
2
3  total = 0
4
5  for index in range(1, 8):
6
7    print("")
8    temp = int(input("Enter a value between -20 and 60: "))
9
10 while (temp < -20) or (temp > 60):
11   print("")
12   temp = int(input("You must enter a value between -20 and 60. Try again: "))
13
14 total = total + temp
15
16 print("")
17 print("The average temperature was: ", total / 7)
```

- **Normal data** should be spread throughout the range and should cover both positive and negative values, so we might want to choose values of –1, 0 and 20 degrees.
- **Extreme data** should be at the boundaries of the permissible range, so we might want to choose values of –20, –19, 59 and 60 degrees.
- **Exceptional data** should be outside the permissible range. It is a good idea to include values that are well outside the range as well as values just outside it, so we might choose something like –273, –21, 61 and 451.

Our complete set of test data is therefore as follows:

Normal	Extreme	Exceptional
–1, 0, 20	–20, –19, 59, 60	–273, –21, 61, 451

Running the program with this test data will produce the following results:

```
Enter a value between -20 and 60: -1

Enter a value between -20 and 60: 0

Enter a value between -20 and 60: 20

Enter a value between -20 and 60: -273

You must enter a value between -20 and 60. Try again: -21

You must enter a value between -20 and 60. Try again: 61

You must enter a value between -20 and 60. Try again: 451

You must enter a value between -20 and 60. Try again: -20

Enter a value between -20 and 60: -19

Enter a value between -20 and 60: 59

Enter a value between -20 and 60: 60

The average temperature was: 14.142857142857142
```

EXAM TIP

Always test boundary conditions carefully. For example, if you want to check that an integer value is >= 16, make sure that 15 is rejected and 16 and 17 are accepted.

Quick Test 16

1. Which type of test data is outside the normal range expected by the program?
2. Which type of test data is at the boundaries of the range expected by the program?
3. Which type of data should a program be able to detect and reject?
4. Which type of data requires most care on the part of the programmer?

Program documentation

Test documentation

It is good practice to keep a record of what testing has been carried out on a program. Apart from anything else, if the program is subsequently amended the same tests can be re-run to ensure that the results remain the same.

The documentation should consist initially of a **test plan**, showing what **test data** is to be used and what the **expected results** are. Once the tests have been run we can convert the test plan to a **test log** by adding the **actual results** and any **comments**.

Program ID: 2.8	Programmer: A Bunyuck			Date: 1/12/2012
Test No.	**Test Data**	**Expected Result**	**Actual Result**	**Comments**
1	−1	accepted	accepted	
2	0	accepted	accepted	
3	20	accepted	accepted	
4	−273	rejected	rejected	

Comments could include any problems encountered when running the program and the steps taken to resolve them.

EXAM TIP

Testing documentation from previous versions can help us to check that changes to a program haven't introduced any undesirable side effects.

Internal documentation

We have already seen how **comments** can be used to add explanatory text to your programs. Python comments start with a hash sign (#) – other programming languages use different conventions. For example, in C comments start with /* and end with */. In Basic comments start with REM, an abbreviated form of REMARK.

Comments can contain any characters and can use as many lines as necessary. They are solely for the benefit of human readers and will be ignored completely by the computer. Internal documentation is very popular amongst programmers as it cannot be lost and is readily available to anyone amending the code.

Comments can help you to remember why you did something in a particular way if you come back to a program some time later. They are also useful to anyone else who has to amend your code at a later stage. You should be aware that in real life programs are often written by large teams of programmers and it is commonplace to see a programmer modifying code originally written by someone else.

If your programs are well written they should be almost self-documenting, so it should not be necessary to add a comment to every line of code. For example, the use of **meaningful variable names** makes programs easier to read. However, it is useful to comment on lines where the code is not obvious or straightforward.

Useful types of comments include:

- **Program identification:** at the start of a program. This should include the program name and/or ID, the programmer's name and the date written.
- **Prefacing:** short explanatory text at the start of each major subsection of the program.
- **Revision history:** details of changes made to the program, including reasons for change, name of programmer and date completed.
- **Tagging:** explicit marking of the end of constructs, such as loops and if statements.

Good practice

- Use revision history comments to show why and when a change was made.
- Make your comments while you are coding – don't leave it until afterwards, otherwise it won't get done.
- Keep your comments short and simple.
- Use comments to 'prevent' or 'allow' lines of code from being executed during debugging, for example printing intermediate values of variables that won't appear in the final output.

Bad practice

- Don't underestimate your audience. Anyone reading your comments is likely to be a programmer and doesn't need every simple thing explained.
- Don't over-comment. Restrict yourself to aspects that require explanation.
- Don't leave 'commented out' debugging code in the final program. If it is no longer required, delete it.

EXAM TIP

Good internal documentation should provide an 'audit trail' of everything that has happened during the lifespan of a program.

Continues over page ⟶

GOT IT? ☐ ☐ ☐

The following example shows a well-commented program. It is over-simplified and over-commented, but it should give you some idea of how comments can be used effectively.

```
 1  # Program 2.8: Odd or Even
 2
 3  # Programmer   : A Bunyuck
 4  # Date Written: 12/12/2012
 5
 6  # This Program reads an integer number between 0 and 999
 7  # and decides whether it is odd or even.
 8  # Numbers outside the permitted range will be rejected
 9
10  # Get an integer number
11
12  number = int(input("Enter an integer number between 0 and 999: "))
13
14  # Check that number entered lies between 0 and 999
15
16  while ((number < 0) or (number > 999)):
17      number = int(input("You must enter an integer number (0 to 999). Try again: "))
18  # End while loop
19
20  # Use mod(%) to decide whether number is odd or even.
21  # If the remainder is 1 the number is odd.
22  # If the remainder is 0 the number is even.
23
24  if (number % 2 == 1):
25      print(number, "is an odd number")
26  else:
27      print(number, "is an even number")
28  # End if
29
30  # End of program
```

Quick Test 17

1. What is the name of the document that describes what tests we intend to carry out on a program and the expected results?

2. What is the name of the document that describes what happens while we are testing a program?

3. What should happen to any debugging code that has been included in a program when the final version is produced?

4. Why should we avoid being over-detailed in program comments?

5. What information should be included in the program identification comments?

Editing features 1: IDLE

Python

We've already made some use of the editing features of one particular Python programming environment, the **IDLE Graphical Use Interface (GUI)** as implemented in Windows. Other implementations, such as Linux, function in a very similar manner. In this section we're going to look at it in a bit more detail and then compare it with a totally different environment, **App Inventor**.

IDLE stands for 'Integrated Development Environment'. It was named by Guido van Rossum, the original developer of Python. Python is said to be named after the TV comedy show Monty Python, so the name IDLE may also refer to one of the stars, Eric Idle. IDLE is itself written in Python and has been supplied with Windows and Linux versions since some of the earliest releases.

The main features of IDLE are:

- interactive operation
- a multi-window text editor with syntax highlighting, auto-completion and smart indent
- Python Shell with syntax highlighting
- integrated debugger

IDLE can be started by selecting it under Python 3.3 in the Start menu.

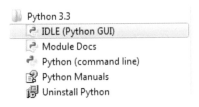

It starts in the main window, the Python Shell:

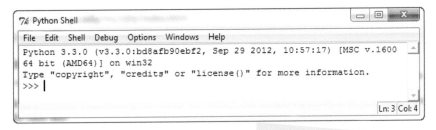

55

One feature we haven't examined so far is interactive use of the Python Shell. Many commands will simply execute directly if typed in:

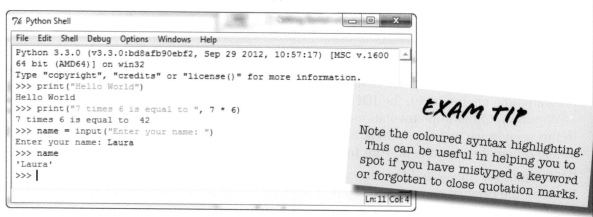

If you want to write a program, choose **File, New Window** from the menu and an editing window will open:

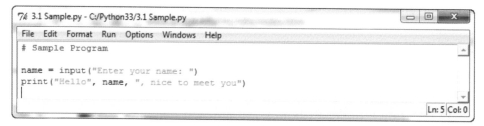

To run the program choose **Run** and then **Run Module** from the menu:

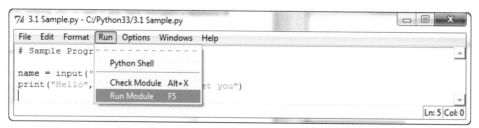

The output is as follows:

```
Enter your name: Laura
Hello Laura , nice to meet you
```

Continues over page ⟶

Let's look at a simple Python program to read two numbers and calculate their average. Later we'll have a look at how the same program could be implemented in App Inventor. The program and its output are shown below:

```python
# Read in two numbers and calculate average

Num1 = float(input("Enter the first number: "))
Num2 = float(input("Enter the second number: "))

Sum = Num1 + Num2
Avg = Sum / 2

print("")
print("The average is: ", Avg)
```

```
Enter the first number: 23
Enter the second number: 15

The average is:  19.0
```

Quick Test 18

1. What are the two main components of IDLE?
2. What feature of IDLE helps locate typing errors?
3. How do you run a program in Python?

Editing features 2: App Inventor

App Inventor was originally developed by Hal Abelson of **Massachusetts Institute of Technology (MIT)**, while on secondment to **Google**. It was based on an earlier programming environment named Scratch. When Abelson returned to MIT, the project moved back with him, and App Inventor is now maintained there. App Inventor is used for producing applications for Android devices, such as smartphones and tablets. It allows us to produce applications using a drag-and-drop graphical environment similar to Scratch. Full details can be obtained at http://appinventor.mit.edu/. Google offers a similar programming environment known as **Blockly**.

During development, App inventor programs can be run on an Android device, which can be connected via USB or WiFi, or on an emulator supplied with the package. The emulator runs on your computer and behaves just like an Android phone. Completed versions can be installed as Apps on Android devices.

Log on to App Inventor by pointing your browser to: *http://appinventor.mit.edu/*

| Teach | Explore | Invent |
| Educator Resources | Information & Tutorials | Create Mobile Apps |

EXAM TIP

You'll need a recent version of Java installed on your computer to use App Inventor.

Click on the ***Invent*** button. You'll be asked to sign in using a Gmail address – if you don't already have a Gmail account you'll need to create one. After signing in you'll be asked to give App Inventor permission to access your Gmail account.

App Inventor has two major components: the App Inventor Designer and the App Inventor Blocks Editor. The App Inventor Designer lets you select components for your app and specify properties such as titles, sizes, orientation, colours, etc. The designer is a Windows application, but both the blocks editor and the emulator are Java applications.

The following screenshots show the construction of a simple application that produces a barking sound when a picture of a dog is clicked.

The **App Inventor Blocks Editor** is where you assemble program blocks specifying how the components should behave. Programs are assembled by dragging and dropping blocks, fitting them together like pieces of a jigsaw puzzle.

Continues over page ⟶

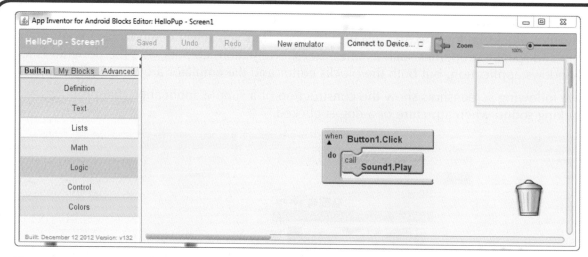

Your app appears on the phone or emulator step-by-step as you build it, so you can test your work as you go. When you're done, you can package your app and produce a stand-alone application that can be installed on any Android phone.

Now let's look at how our simple program to calculate the average of two numbers could be implemented in App Inventor. First, we set up the screen design. There are two major components, **FirstNum** and **SecondNum**, each of which contains a label and a text box. Below these are a **Calculate Button** and a space for the **Result** (not visible).

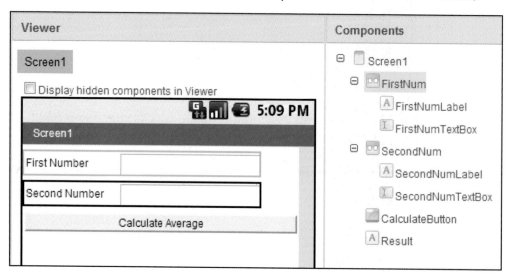

Now we can go to the blocks editor and define the variables needed for our program. There are four of these: **Num1, Num2, Sum** and **Avg**. Each of them is set initially to 0.

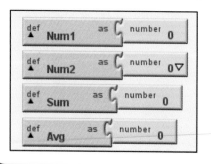

After that, we define the logic needed to specify what happens when the **Calculate** button is clicked:

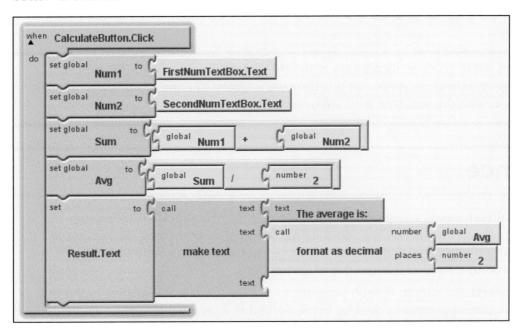

This is fairly straightforward, apart from the last section, where we set the value for the result. To do this, we call a procedure named **make text**, telling it to display the text 'The average is:', followed by the value of Avg, rounded to two decimal places.

Finally, we can display the App on our emulator:

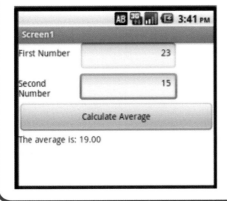

Quick Test 19

1. What is the main difference between the programming environments used in Python and App Inventor?
2. Where is App Inventor now supported?
3. Where can App Inventor programs be run?
4. What are the two main components of App Inventor?
5. How can an Android phone connect to App Inventor?

Standard constructs: sequence and selection

In this section we're going to look again at the three standard programming constructs, sequence, selection and iteration, but this time we're going to compare the way they are used in Python with the way that they are used in **App Inventor**.

Sequence

As we have already seen, a sequence consists of a series of instructions following one after the other. There is no decision-making, looping, or branching. Many simple programs, particularly those that are only designed to carry out a single task each time they are executed, consist of a sequence of instructions.

Earlier, we looked at a simple Python program to display the first five entries in the five times table. A similar program could be implemented in App Inventor as shown below. (Only 5 × 1 and 5 × 2 have been shown in the blocks editor to save space.)

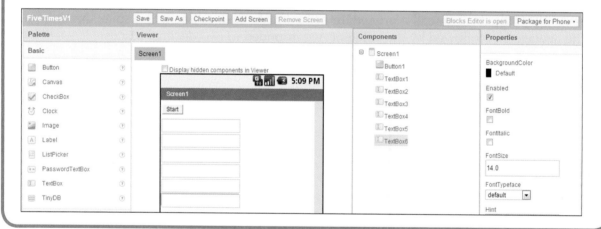

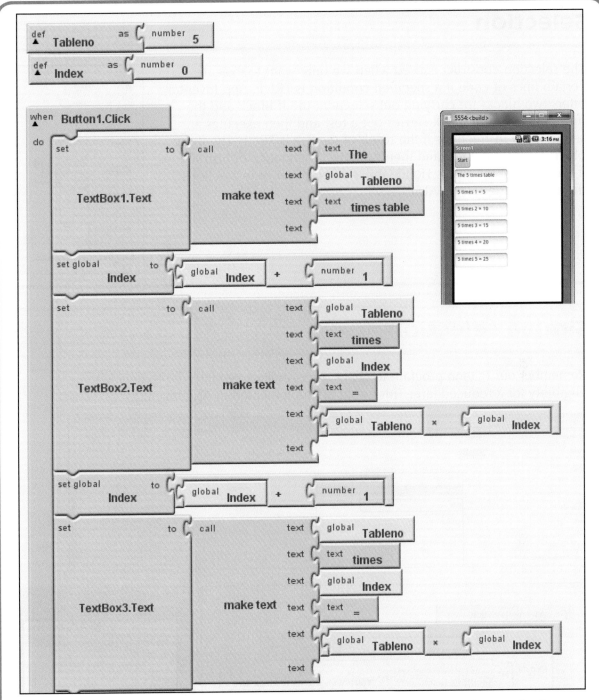

Although this accomplishes the objective of displaying the five times table, it is far from the most effective way of doing so as it involves repetition of similar statements.

Selection

The selection construct is used when we only want to execute certain lines of code if a specified condition is TRUE. App Inventor offers two blocks for carrying out selection: the **if block** and the **ifelse block**. The **if block** carries out a test and then executes a sequence of instructions if the result of the test is TRUE. The **ifelse block** carries out a test and then executes a sequence of instructions if the result of the test is TRUE, and a different set of instructions if the result of the test is FALSE.

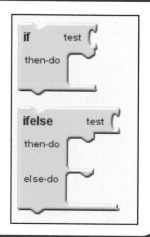

Simple selection

Remember our Python program to check a passenger's age in order to decide their eligibility for a reduced fare? This could be implemented in App Inventor:

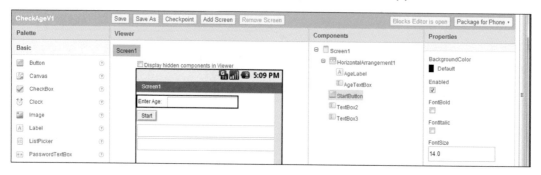

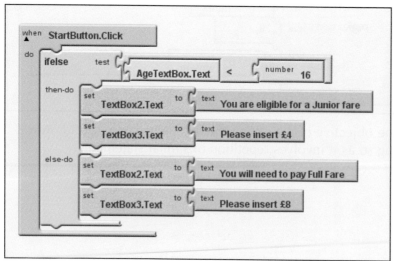

EXAM TIP

Simple selections are implemented in App Inventor using if blocks and ifelse blocks.

Complex selection

More complex selections can be accomplished in App Inventor simply by nesting one ifelse block inside another. This can be done to as many levels as necessary, allowing very complex selections to be handled. Let's look at how the above program can be amended to deal with the situation where passengers over the age of 59 are also entitled to a reduced fare. The designer is unchanged, but the blocks editor and sample output will now look as follows:

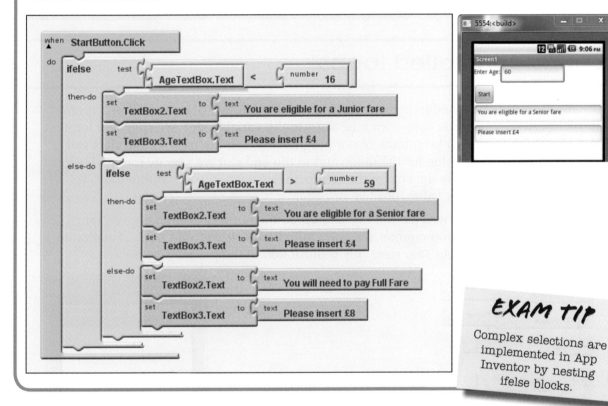

EXAM TIP

Complex selections are implemented in App Inventor by nesting ifelse blocks.

Quick Test 20

1. What does the if block in App Inventor do?
2. What does the ifelse block in App Inventor do?
3. How are complex selections handled in App Inventor?

Standard constructs: iteration

As we have already noted, we often encounter situations where groups of instructions need to be repeated. This is known as **iteration** and is implemented using loops.

Like Python, and most other programming languages, App Inventor offers two different types of loops: **count-controlled loops** (using the **for range block**) and **condition-controlled loops** (using the **while block**).

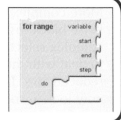

Count-controlled loops

The **for range block** is used to do something a specific number of times within a given range. We need to provide values for four slots. In the **variable slot**, we specify a loop counter, which is used to keep track of our progress through the loop. In the **start slot**, we specify the starting value for the range and in the **end slot** we specify the final value. In the **step slot** we specify the size of the step between each iteration of the loop. This is often 1, but it can be any value, positive or negative.

Consider the situation where we want to add up all the numbers within a given range. We'll use **Index** as our loop counter variable, **InitialValue** as our start value, **FinalValue** as our end value and 1 as our step size. This is illustrated in the program below:

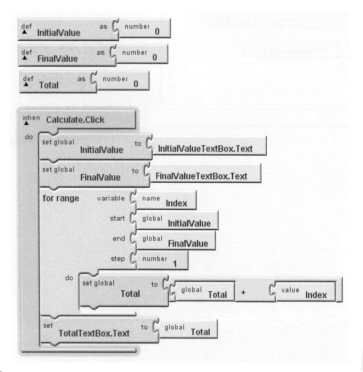

EXAM TIP

Note that the App Inventor **for range block** works in a slightly different manner from the Python **for loop.** We need only supply the required final value – not a value one greater as required by Python.

Condition-controlled loops

Condition-controlled loops are used when we wish to execute a group of statements repeatedly until a specified condition occurs, rather than executing them a fixed number of times. They are implemented in App Inventor by means of the **while block**.

The simple program below accepts the number Ceiling and then calculates and prints the sum of all the numbers from 1 up to Ceiling. The value of Ceiling is entered and the user then clicks the Sum Number button, after which the while loop carries out the required calculation.

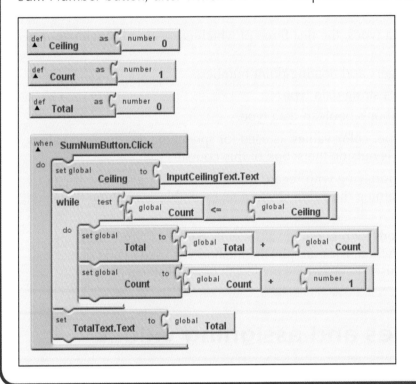

Quick Test 21

1. What four values need to be provided in an App Inventor for range block?
2. Which type of block does App Inventor use for count-controlled loops?
3. Which type of block does App Inventor use for condition-controlled loops?
4. What values can the step slot in a for range loop take?

Data types and operators

We have already seen that Python has four distinct data types:

- **Integer:** used for whole numbers.
- **Float:** use for numbers with a fractional part (floating-point numbers).
- **Boolean:** can only store the values True or False.
- **String:** used to store character data.

A fifth data type, **complex numbers**, is outside the scope of this course.

App Inventor has four basic data types, the first three of which correspond roughly to the Python data types:

- **Number:** used for both integers and floating-point numbers.
- **Text:** corresponds to Python's string data type.
- **Boolean:** corresponds to Python's boolean data type.

The fourth App Inventor data type, **color values**, is used for specifying the numeric values related to different colours and is outside the scope of this course.

In general App Inventor is very forgiving with regard to data types. For example, if you try to add a number variable, containing the value '2', to a text variable containing the value '4', you will get away with it.

Each data type has its own **methods** for processing values of its own data type – these are similar to the operators used in Python. For example, the method + is used to add numeric values and the method **length** is used to determine the length of a text string.

> **EXAM TIP**
>
> App Inventor does not distinguish between integer and floating-point data types. Both are covered by the number data type.

Defining variables and assigning values

We can define variables and give them names by selecting the **def variable as** block under **Built-In/Definition** in the blocks editor. We can then give them an initial value (which defines the type of the variable) by choosing the appropriate block from the **Text, Math** or **Logic** block group under **Built-In**.

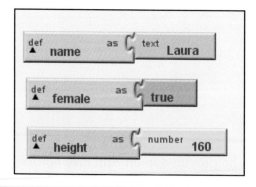

Numerical operations

We can use the numerical operation methods in the Math block group to carry out the usual calculations such as addition (+), subtraction (−), multiplication (×) and division (/).

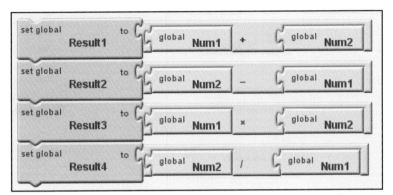

The result of the calculation can be assigned to a variable.

EXAM TIP

Numerical and comparison operation methods are found in the Math block group.

Comparison operations

We can use the comparison operation methods in the Math block group to carry out the usual comparisons, such as greater than (>), less than (<), greater than or equal to (>=), less than or equal to (<=), equal to (=) or not equal to (not=).

The boolean result of the comparison can be assigned to a variable.

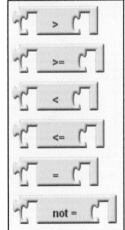

Quick Test 22

1. What App Inventor feature corresponds to operators in Python?

2. What type of result does a comparison produce in App Inventor?

3. How are variables defined in App Inventor?

4. Where can numerical and comparison operation methods be found in App Inventor?

Mathematical functions

App Inventor provides a wide range of mathematical functions. The main ones are as follows:

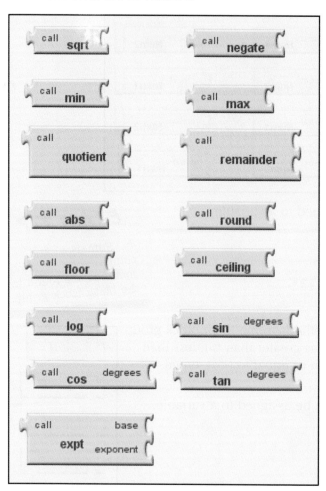

- **sqrt:** returns the square root of the given number.
- **negate:** returns the negative of the given number.
- **min:** returns the smallest value in a given set of numbers.
- **max:** returns the largest value in a given set of numbers.
- **quotient:** returns the result of dividing the first number by the second and discarding the fractional part of the result.

- **remainder:** returns the result of dividing the first given number by the second and taking the remainder.
- **abs:** returns the absolute value of the given number.
- **round:** rounds the given number to the nearest integer and returns the result; if the number is halfway between two integers, it rounds to the even integer.
- **floor:** calculates the greatest integer that is less than or equal to the given number.
- **ceiling:** returns the smallest integer that is greater than or equal to the given number.
- **log:** returns the natural logarithm of the given number.
- **sin:** returns the sine of the given number (in degrees).
- **cos:** returns the cosine of the given number (in degrees).
- **tan:** returns the tangent of the given number (in degrees).
- **expt:** raises the first given number to the power of the second and returns the result.

> **EXAM TIP**
>
> Note that the App Inventor trig functions work in degrees, unlike the Python trig functions, which work in radians.

Quick Test 23

1. What is the difference between the App Inventor round and floor functions?
2. What happens if you try to round a number that is exactly halfway between the integers above and below it?
3. What units are used by default for the App Inventor trig functions?

Translation and execution of high-level code 1

Although it is much easier for humans to write computer programs in a high-level language such as Python or Java, computers can only deal with programs written in their native language: **machine code**, also called binary code or object code.

Each type of processor has its own specific machine code. Most PCs use Intel or AMD (Advanced Micro Devices) processors. These are very similar and execute the same machine code. However, most mobile devices use ARM (Advanced Research Machines) processors, which run a completely different type of machine code.

The Intel/AMD processors belong to a category known as **complex instruction set computers (CISC)**. They have hundreds of complex machine code instructions, so a single instruction can handle almost any requirement that may occur. ARM processors belong to a category known as **reduced instruction set computers (RISC)**. They have a relatively small number of simple machine code instructions, which can execute very rapidly. When complex instructions are required they are created by combining simpler instructions.

All high-level language programs must be translated into machine code before they can be executed. There are two different approaches to translation. **Compilers** translate a complete program into a standalone machine code program that can then be executed, while **interpreters** translate a program line-by-line and execute each line as soon as it is translated. Both approaches have their advantages and disadvantages – we will look at these in more detail shortly.

People sometimes try to classify programming languages as compiled or interpreted, but in practice most programming languages can be translated by either method. However, languages are often written with a particular implementation in mind, so some languages may be biased towards a particular type of translation, for example C was designed to be compiled whereas Java was designed to be interpreted. However, that does not mean that Java compilers or C interpreters do not exist.

EXAM TIP

Compilers and interpreters are processor-specific. A compiler and/or an interpreter must be written for each type of processor that a program is expected to run on.

Compilers

As we have already noted, a compiler takes a complete program as input and translates it into an equivalent machine code program. This process is known as compilation and can be broken down into four stages: lexical analysis, syntactical analysis, code generation and optimisation.

In the **lexical analysis** stage the compiler analyses the source code, input as a stream of characters, and tries to recognise entities that are meaningful in terms of the programming language. For example, the input

```
avg = (num1 + num2) / 2
```

might be recognised as consisting of:

<variable>

<assignment operator>

<open bracket>

<variable>

<addition operator>

<variable>

<close bracket>

<division operator>

<number>

During the **syntactical analysis** stage the compiler attempts to turn the recognised entities into instructions that are meaningful in terms of the grammar of the programming language. For example, it might decide that the example given above means: 'add the second variable to the third variable and divide the sum by two, placing the result in the first variable'.

During the **code generation** phase, the compiler attempts to produce a machine code program that will carry out the required instructions.

Once these steps have been carried out for each line of the program, a complete machine code program can be produced. Once this has been done the compiler enters the **optimisation** phase, where it tries to ensure that the generated code is as efficient as possible.

Quick Test 24

1. Which type of processor has a small number of machine code instructions that can be executed very rapidly?

2. During which stage of the compilation process does the compiler analyse the source code and try to recognise entities that are meaningful in terms of the programming language?

3. Programming languages can be classified as compiled or interpreted. True or false?

4. What is the final stage of the compilation process?

Translation and execution of high-level code 2

Interpreters

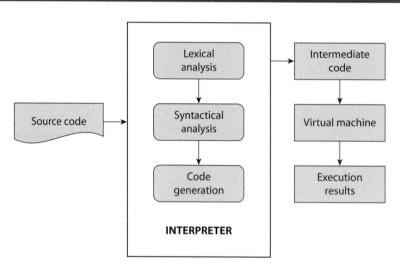

An interpreter operates on a line-by-line basis, going through the lexical analysis, syntactical analysis and code generation phases in a similar manner to a compiler, but in this case, rather than generating machine code for a real machine, the code generation phase produces an **intermediate code**, sometimes referred to as **Bytecode**. This intermediate code is the machine code for an **abstract** or **virtual machine**, i.e. a computer program that emulates the operation of a real computer.

The code is then executed on the virtual machine and the interpreter moves on to process the next line. Note that, unlike a compiler, an interpreter cannot carry out optimisation as it never has access to the whole program – each line is executed as soon as it has been translated.

EXAM TIP

Interpreted code is executed on a virtual machine.

Advantages and disadvantages

Both compilers and interpreters have their own advantages and disadvantages – some of these are listed in the tables below.

COMPILERS	
Advantages	**Disadvantages**
All errors can be found in a single pass. Generated code is highly optimised and runs efficiently. Once the program has been compiled it can be executed many times without recompiling.	Errors can't be found until a program is complete and ready for compilation. Compilation of large programs can take a long time. If anything is changed, the whole program needs to be recompiled.

INTERPRETERS	
Advantages	**Disadvantages**
Errors can be located during program development. Programs can be run again as soon as they are amended – no need to recompile.	Programs generally stop after the first error is encountered, so it may take several runs to find them all. Execution time is slow in comparison to compiled code. Programs cannot be optimised.

EXAM TIP

The best of all possible worlds is to have both a compiler and an interpreter available for the same language. The interpreter can be used during program development and then, once the program is completed and debugged, it can be compiled to produce a fast and efficient version for regular use.

Quick Test 25

1. Why can't interpreters carry out optimisation in the same way as compilers?
2. What type of code is generated by an interpreter?
3. What is a virtual machine?
4. Why are interpreters preferred over compilers for program development?

Structures and links 1

What are information systems?

An information system is a combination of hardware and software that stores information people can access and manipulate. Databases are an information system, and form the backbone of many websites. Companies like Amazon and eBay are huge online databases that can be searched for items for sale. A great deal of work goes into how these systems are created and maintained. This unit looks at considerations for designing and creating an information system.

Database structure

Flat file

A flat file database is a database with only one table. The table is made up of **fields** and **records**. A field holds a single piece of data such as a name, address or age. A record is all of the related data about one person or thing, such as someone's medical record, or car. All the data on the **one topic** is called a **flat file**.

Limitations

There are limitations to using flat file databases.

- **Data duplication** can occur if the same item of data is stored more than once in different tables.
- **Data inconsistency** happens when a change is made to one piece of data in one table, but not updated in another where it is stored. The data can no longer be relied on, causing data integrity issues.

Linked tables

A database made up of multiple linked tables is known as a **relational database**. Each table has its own unique **primary key field**.

Advantages

There are advantages to using linked tables when designing a database. Each item of data is only stored once. This makes sure that only one data item is used. Data integrity is maintained and data duplication is avoided.

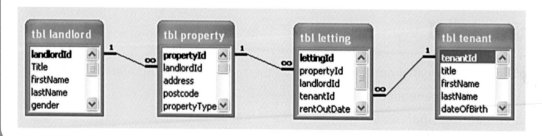

Primary key

Every row in a table needs to be **unique**. The **primary key** is a unique item of data used to identify a row. It is used to make **relationships** between tables.

Here are some rules for a primary key.

- It has to be unique.
- It cannot be left empty.
- It should be constant over time, for example an address would not be suitable because it might change.

Foreign key

A **foreign key** is when one of the database tables is a key from another table that refers to a specific key, usually the primary key. A primary key can be targeted by multiple foreign keys from other tables.

Field types

When you set up a new table in a database, you have to specify the fields that you require, select the appropriate data types and the field properties. Data is stored in different ways, and this helps check for the wrong type of data being entered by the user and makes sure the data is stored as efficiently as possible by the system.

Field type	Main characteristics
Text	Allows text, numbers and symbols
Numbers	Whole numbers or decimal
Date	Accepts only dates
Time	Accepts time formats 18:21, 6:21 pm
Graphics	Used for images
Calculated	Performs calculations on text, number, date and time
Data	Is a result of a formula
Link	A reference to a file stored outside the database
Boolean	Used when field value has one or two states: yes/no, on/off true/false

	A	B	C	D	E	F
1	First name	Surname	DOB	email		
2	Flynn	Hansen	31/10/86	In.scelerisque@nequenonquam.org		
3	Quail	Dillon	21/06/83	imperdiet@NulladignissimMaecenas.ca		
4	Basia	Donaldson	08/03/95	ac@magnaNam.ca		
5	Raja	Stephens	15/06/81	eget@miAliquamgravida.org		
6	Chadwick	Vincent	07/05/80	mi.lorem.vehicula@dis.edu		
7	April	Church	05/07/99	egestas.Sed.pharetra@luctusvulputate.org		
8	Cruz	Fernandez	25/10/93	eget.volutpat@Donecnibh.org		
9	Vance	Booth	19/01/00	ac.orci@etipsumcursus.ca		
10	Tatum	Lester	02/02/88	odio.semper@necmalesuada.org		

Field length and range

Sometimes it is important to set the field length and field range so that the database is **efficient**, i.e. not using more resources than necessary.

Field size

This should be set to a sensible value for the data that is being stored. For example, a surname is not likely to need more than 30 characters. You shouldn't leave this at the default of 255 characters.

Field range

This is where you can set a **validation rule** for that field. For example, >=1 AND <=6. Any numbers entered in this field that are not in the range of between 1 and 6 inclusive are rejected.

EXAM TIP

When creating a database, try setting the field size and range to different values, and note what happens when data entered is not valid.

Quick Test 26

1. What is an information system?
2. What are two limitations of a flat file database?
3. What is a relational database?
4. What is a primary key?
5. What is the difference between field size and field range?

Structures and links 2

Websites

A **website** is a collection of **webpages** and **hyperlinks**. Websites allow us to watch TV, catch up on the news, buy almost anything, and even socialise. We are living more and more of our lives online, and this is only set to increase as Internet connections get faster and cheaper. It is important to know how websites are constructed, and how they are used as information systems in today's world.

URL

A uniform resource locator (**URL**) is the name given to the **web address** of a site. The URL of the BBC website is: http://www.bbc.co.uk. Each page on a site has its own URL. For example http://www.bbc.co.uk/news/ is the URL for the BBC website for news and http://www.bbc.co.uk/weather/2650225 is the URL for weather in the Dundee area on the BBC site.

Hyperlinks

A **hyperlink** is what makes a website work. It is the part that, when clicked, takes the user to another page or website. If you have used webpages before, you have used hyperlinks. There are two types of hyperlinks you need to know about.

- An **internal hyperlink** is a link which points to a particular part of a page, or to another page on the **same website**.
- An **external hyperlink** is a hyperlink that connects you to **another website.**

Continues over page ⟶

Navigation

Navigation within a website or any information system is how the screens or pages are linked together, so the user can move from one place to another to get around the system. There are three ways the **sequence** of information can be linked.

- **Linear**: screens or pages are linked in a sequence, one after the other.

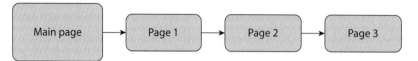

- **Hierarchical**: screens or pages are grouped together by topic and are accessed from the main page.

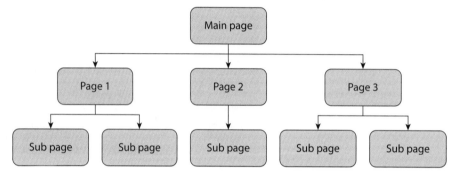

- **Web**: screens or pages can be accessed in any order as links exist between all pages.

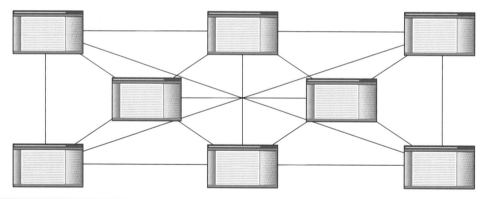

Quick Test 27

1. What is a website?
2. What is the difference between an internal and external hyperlink?
3. What does URL stand for?
4. Name one navigation structure used in creating websites.

User interface

When designing an information system, whether it is a database or a website, it is of upmost importance that the user interface is designed so that the user will feel comfortable with it. Most systems will use a graphical user interface (GUI).

A GUI uses a pointing device (a mouse) and graphical objects (icons) to allow the user to issue instructions to the software. The user interface is the way a user and the system communicate and interact. There are a few elements that you need to take into consideration when designing the user interface.

Visual layout

The visual layout of an information system is how the software looks. The **colours** used in the system, for example, need to be **consistent** and relevant to the subject. The primary goal of any layout is for it to be clearly organised, free from clutter and allow users to locate information.

Readability

In order to be useful any information must be readable. **Readability** means a good design and page layout. All information systems must obey these principles. If the data within a system is not presented in a way that is easily read and visually appealing then the chances of retaining the interest and attention of the user are reduced.

Navigation

The navigation of a system is how the user makes their way around the pages and locates information. **Icons, navigation bars** or **menus** are the most common way of allowing a user to navigate. It is important that the navigation is simple to understand for all users. To be effective the navigation of a system or website needs to be consistent throughout and requires minimal clicking to get to where the visitor wants to go.

Consistency

Any system that is designed needs to have a consistent layout. All the pages should use the same **font**, **text size** and **colours**. The same settings should be used for **headings** and **sub-headings**. It looks more professional if there is a consistent approach to the design of a system or website.

EXAM TIP

Look at the BBC website, and note how the look of all the pages is consistent. They have the same fonts, colours, etc. This is a well-designed, professional-looking site.

Interactivity

Sometimes users want to be able to interact with websites and information systems. It is not enough just to read information from them. An example of **interactivity** on a website could be allowing a user to not only look at images of mobile phones for sale, but interact with the image of each phone. The user can move the cursor over the mobile phone and the entire angle of the phone changes and rotates.

Quick Test 28

1. What type of user interface do most information systems use?
2. What is the primary goal of an information system layout?
3. Why should an information system have a consistent layout?
4. What are the most common ways to navigate round an information system or website?

Media types 1

File storage

There are many different ways to store files, but choosing the correct one can reduce the amount of backing storage needed. Some file types compress data, which allows the file to be transferred faster over a network. We experience this benefit when downloading files from the Internet. The smaller the file, the faster it will download.

There are two compression techniques you need to know about: **lossy** and **lossless**.

Compression techniques

- **Lossy:** when a file is compressed using this technique, **data is lost** during the process. Sometimes the loss of data is not noticeable, but the more a file is compressed using this technique the more noticeable the loss of data becomes.

- **Lossless:** when a file is compressed using a lossless technique, **no data is lost** during the process. Lossless compression is used in cases where it is important that the original and the decompressed data are identical, such as executable programs or text files.

File types

Text

- **txt:** this is a standard text document that contains **unformatted text** – it is recognised by any word processing and text editing software packages. Various hardware devices, such as smartphones and E-readers, recognise plain text files.

- **RTF (rich text format):** is a common text file format. It supports **several types of text formatting**, such as bold, italics, different fonts and font sizes. RTFs can also save images that are included in the text file.

Audio

- **WAV (waveform audio file format):** this is a digital audio file format used for storing waveform data. It is usually uncompressed, but can use lossless compression. Audio can be saved with **different sampling rates** and **different bit rates**, usually 44.1 KHz, 16 bit, and stereo format (CD quality).

- **MP3:** a compressed audio format that produces near CD quality sound in a file roughly 10% the size of a WAV file. The MP3 format is very popular because of the high quality to low file size ratio. It uses lossy compression, where audio that the human ear cannot detect is removed first. This reduces the file size significantly, but not the quality.

Quick Test 29

1. Name a sound file format that uses lossy compression.
2. Why do some files need to be compressed?
3. What compression technique does not lose data during the process?
4. What type of compression does MP3 use?
5. What text file is capable of storing text formatting?

Media types 2

Graphics

- **JPEG (Joint Photographic Experts Group):** is a graphic format that can support up to **24-bit** colour (true colour). JPEGs are good for storing digital images. JPEGs use lossy compression. The level of compression can be adjusted.

- **BMP (bitmap):** a bitmap is made up of a grid of pixels. The pixels of a black and white image are stored as 1s and 0s. Each pixel is 1 bit in size. Colour bitmap images can be very large in size, as each pixel can contain different colour depths. The higher the colour depth, the more colours that pixels can represent. Bitmaps are uncompressed, and may require a lot of backing storage.

- **GIF (graphics interchange format):** GIF is based on an **8-bit** colour code meaning that it is capable of representing a maximum of 256 colours. Because of this limitation, GIFs are used mainly for charts, cartoons, navigation buttons in websites, etc. GIF uses a **lossless** compression technique, and can support transparency so that part of an image can blend into the background. GIFs can also be animated (animated gif).

- **PNG (portable network graphic):** contains a bitmap of indexed colours and uses **lossless** compression, similar to a GIF file commonly used to store graphics for web images. While GIF images only support fully opaque or fully transparent pixels, PNG images allow the image colours to fade from opaque to transparent.

Video

- **MPEG (Moving Picture Experts Group):** MPEG files are popular video files. They are compressed by cutting out any unchanged data from frames in the video (lossy compression). When an MPEG video is played back, it is uncompressed, meaning the viewer does not notice the difference.

- **AVI (audio video interleave):** AVI is what is known as a multimedia container file. It stores the video and audio data in a single file, and is not compressed. This limits the quality of the video and audio that can be stored.

PDF (portable document format) files

PDFs were created by Adobe and work on multiple platforms. They are used for attachments in e-mails, or for saving documents in a standard format for viewing on different computer systems. They can **contain text, images, graphs,** etc. and appear exactly the same on screen as they will when printed. Google and other search engines now index PDF documents, allowing users to search for them online. They can be viewed online using Adobe Reader plug-in.

Quick Test 30

1. What video file uses lossy compression?
2. How many bits can JPEG images support?
3. What are the pixels of a black and white bitmap stored as?
4. Name three standard file formats for graphics.

Factors affecting file size and quality

The storage size and the quality of a file depend on a number of factors. Graphics files will be affected by the **resolution** of the image and the **colour depth** of the image. Sound files will be affected by the **sampling rate** of the sound as well as the **sample depth**. The larger the files you have in your information system, the more storage space you will need. A website that has lots of high-quality images will also take more time to download.

Resolution

Resolution is the measure of the size of the pixels in an image. High-resolution graphics have a large number of small pixels. Low-resolution images have a small number of large pixels. A high-resolution graphic is of a better quality, but requires more storage space. Resolution is usually measured in dots per inch (DPI).

Colour depth

EXAM TIP

Digital cameras store photographs using 24-bit colour depth. This is called True Colour.

The colour depth is the number of bits used to store the colour of each pixel. The higher the colour depth, the more colours can be represented, thus improving the quality of an image.

Image type	Bit depth	Colours	File size for an image 3" × 3" at a resolution of 600 dpi
Black and white	1 bit	2 colours	395.5 KB
GIF	8 bit	256 colours	3.08 MB
JPEG	24 bit	16.7 million colours	9.26 MB

A high colour depth graphic is of a better quality, but requires more storage space.

Sampling rate

This is the number of samples per second in a sound file. The higher the sampling rate, the better the quality of sound, as there are more samples of the sound taken per second. A common sample rate of CD quality sound is 44.1KHz. That is 44,100 samples per second.

Compression

Compression is needed with graphic and sound files to reduce the storage size required. However, by compressing a file, we also reduce the quality of that file. There is a trade-off between quality and file size.

When designing an information system it is important not to have files that are taking up too much space, but equally if the system is, for example, a website selling something, then the pictures need to be of good quality. There are two types of compression you need to know about: **lossy** and **lossless**.

Lossy compression

This type of compression removes some of the data in a file and only keeps what is deemed necessary. In a graphic for example, colours and shades that humans cannot differentiate between are removed first. If we kept on compressing the file, there would be a noticeable reduction in quality as more colours and shades are removed. MPEG, JPEG and MP3 all use lossy compression.

Lossless compression

No data is lost when a file is compressed. It does this by using a code to store patterns of bits that occur repeatedly throughout the file. GIF uses this type of compression.

> **EXAM TIP**
>
> Know which type of compression is used with different files.

Quick Test 31

1. How many colours can a GIF store?
2. What is resolution, and what is it measured in?
3. What is the bit depth used in a JPEG?
4. What is sampling?
5. Why do we need to compress graphic and sound files?

Purpose, features, functionality and users

Purpose

A business or an organisation needs to have a strategy in place that will guide the purchase, installation, support and training needed for any information system that they will use. If there is no clear strategy, then serious difficulties may be encountered – applications may not work, staff may not have the required training or expertise, and the system may not be fit for purpose.

Fitness for purpose

When making a decision about the type of information system to use, it is important to consider if it will be **fit for purpose**. This involves asking how well the product performs the function for which it was designed. There are several ways we can consider if a system is fit for purpose:

- range of data objects
- formatting functions
- range of operations
- human computer interface
- online help and online tutorial

EXAM TIP

Look at a website or a system in school and note down what it is supposed to do. Look at what it does and try to think of ways it could be improved.

Users

When designing or choosing an information system, one of the most important things to consider is who will be using the system. It's no use designing a system for one group of people and then expecting the same design to be successful with a completely different group doing different tasks in a different setting.

The type of user and the age range of the users are worth noting when designing a system, especially the user interface, as in previous pages.

Expert users

Expert users can normally type quickly and are familiar with using keyboard commands or short cuts rather than drop down menus. They are able to memorise commands and key combinations. This saves time, compared to using a mouse and clicking on icons.

Novice users

When considering design for a novice user, it is important to consider a good **human computer interface** (HCI). It has to be intuitive and easy for complete beginners to use and navigate without a great deal of assistance.

A **graphical user interface** (GUI) uses a pointing device and icons to navigate around the system. Most users will be familiar with this environment.

Age range

The age range of the users is another important factor to consider when designing and developing a system. Older people may have diminished vision, varying degrees of hearing loss, hand-eye coordination problems and difficulty with fine motor coordination.

Younger people have grown up with computer technology and are more comfortable using it. They may be familiar with other existing systems, websites and ways to access information, and this is something that could be considered when designing a new information system.

Quick Test 32

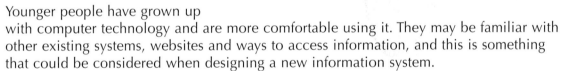

1. What does fit for purpose mean?
2. Who are the two types of user that need to be considered when designing a new system?
3. Why does a business need to have a strategy in place when buying an information system?
4. What is a GUI?

Coding

Scripting languages

When you are developing an information system, it is sometimes essential to tailor the system to the specific needs of the users or desires of the designers. Scripting languages can be used to achieve this. Scripting languages are high-level programming language that is interpreted by another program. Scripting languages can also be embedded within Hypertext mark-up language (HTML) and are used to add functionality to a web page, such as different menu styles or graphic displays or to serve dynamic advertisements. There are two types of scripting language: **client side** and **server side**.

Server-side scripting

Server-side scripting performs all of its processing on the **web server** and delivers a web page to the user's browser. This differs from client-side scripting which does all of the processing on a **user's computer**. It is used mostly to create pull down menus on websites, pop-up windows, and change the mouse icon when it passes over a hyperlink.

Client-side scripting

- JavaScript: this is a common scripting language that you may be familiar with. It is used by web authors to allow them to create dynamic and interactive web content. It is an open language, meaning the source code can be altered by the user, and can be used by anyone without the need for a licence.

- Macros: macros are a feature of application programs that allow a user to record a series of key strokes or mouse clicks to perform repetitive tasks more quickly.

- ASP, PHP and JSP are examples of other scripting languages.

```
<meta http
<meta http-equiv="co...
<title>Document Title</titl
<link rev="made" href="mail
<link rev="start" href="./"
<style type="text/css" medi
    @import "style/base.css";
  ./style>    ~e="text/javascr
               ~javascr
```

Mark-up languages

Mark-up languages are used for the processing and the presentation of text. The mark-up language specifies code used for formatting the layout and the style that is within the text file. These are called tags. Hypertext mark-up language (HTML) is an example of a widely known mark-up language that is used on the web.

HTML

HTML is used to create documents on the web, and uses a variety of tags and attributes. Tags are also used to specify hyperlinks. Here are some examples of common tags within HTML:

- **<HEAD> </HEAD>:** The head part of an HTML document.
- **<BODY> </BODY>:** The body part of an HTML document.
- **<B> </B>:** Content is shown as bold type.
- **<CENTER> </CENTER>:** Content is centred on the page.

> ### EXAM TIP
> Ask your teacher to show you the source code for a website. This will show you all the HTML and scripting languages used in the site.

Quick Test 33

1. What is a scripting language?
2. Name the two different types of scripting languages.
3. What is JavaScript used for?
4. What are mark-up languages used for?

Testing

Testing an information system is essential to make sure that it is working for the purpose it was intended for. Testing is used to ensure that all the components and functions of the system are working, and that each element meets the specified requirements.

There are two specific areas of a system that are tested that you need to know for this course. Do the links and navigation work on the system? And does the system match the user interface design?

Links and navigation

Navigation testing is carried out on an information system to ensure that when a user is working with it they can navigate through the software as intended. All links are tested to ensure that they link to the appropriate part of the system, and that all page transitions work correctly.

Here is a list of some navigation tests that can be performed:

- Check there are no broken links or hyperlinks.
- Check for smooth transitions between screens.
- Check all hyperlinks work correctly.
- Check all links within the application work.

> **EXAM TIP**
>
> Have a look at an information system and write-up what testing you think would have been done for that specific system.

User interface design

Before a user interface UI is created it has to first be designed. This usually involves a drawing or a graphic of what the user should see when using the system. It is important that the UI matches this design. All the screens that a user will come across in the system must been designed in this way. The design will show what each element of the UI should do, and these elements will be tested.

Here is a list of some tests that can be performed:
- Check the layout matches the design.
- Check that the spelling is correct.
- Check scroll functions, audio and video clips run without problems.
- Check that the buttons of the page work.
- Check the texts, fonts, colours and sizes match the original design.

Quick Test 34

1. Why do we need to test an information system?
2. What does navigation testing do?
3. What are two tests that can be carried out under navigation testing?
4. What should the design of a user interface show?
5. Name two tests carried out to check if the user interface matches the design.

Types of computer devices

Types of computers

There are many different types of computer devices today – from the traditional desktop computer, to mobile devices and tablets. Each device has different specifications and it is important to know the technical differences between them.

Super computer

This is the fastest type of computer on the planet. They are very expensive, and are used in scientific institutions such as NASA to perform immense amounts of mathematical calculations. Nuclear research and oil exploration are other industries that would make use of a super computer's ability to process data.

Desktop computer

This type of computer is designed to fit comfortably on a desk. It is the type of computer most common in schools and offices. A typical modern specification of a desktop in 2013 would be:

- 4GB RAM.
- 2.5 GHz Dual Core Processor.
- 500 GB backing storage (usually internal hard drive).

Laptop computer

Laptops are becoming more popular as their power increases and cost comes down. They are light and easily carried around, and provide the same functionality as a desktop computer. They are powered by battery, but they can also be plugged into the mains like a desktop. A typical specification of a modern laptop would be the same as a desktop.

EXAM TIP

Compare your home computer's specification to that of the school. Take note of the important specifications such as processor speed, RAM graphics card and backing storage.

Tablet computer

Tablets have become more and more popular since they became available in the late 2000s. Apple's iPad is probably the most successful tablet on the market at the moment. They are light, easily carried around, and make use of a touch screen to allow the user to enter commands. They are not used for inputting a lot of data as they do not have a physical keyboard like a laptop or desktop. They do have a touch screen virtual keyboard. Tablets are excellent for browsing the web, using with social media and taking photographs with the built-in camera. They come with built-in WiFi, or 3G/4G connectivity.

Tablets do not have hard drives; they use solid state or flash backing storage. They cannot hold as much data as laptops and desktops. A typical specification would be:

- Dual core 1.5GHz processor.
- 512 MB RAM.
- 32–64 GB backing storage (usually flash storage).

Smartphone

These days most people has access to a smartphone or mobile device. They are small, fit in your pocket and allow the user to access the Internet, compose emails, take photographs and video, send text messages and make phone calls. They have the ability to allow the user to download apps that increase the functionality of the device, and allow it to make use of mapping software, games and much more. Some smartphones still make use of a physical keyboard, but others such as HTC, Apple and Samsung devices use onscreen keyboards for input. They are not as powerful as the other types of computer systems, but their size and functionality make them very popular.

Operating systems

An operating system is a program that manages all the hardware and software on a computer system. Examples of operating systems are Microsoft Windows, Google Chrome OS, Linux, which is the backbone of Android, and Mac OS X. Tasks that the operating system carries out are:

- Providing a human computer interface (HCI).
- Saving and loading files on backing storage.
- Performing input and output with peripherals.
- Memory management.
- Error reporting.

Quick Test 35

1. Name three types of computer systems.
2. Why are laptops becoming more popular?
3. What type of backing storage do tablet computers use?
4. What makes smartphones so popular?
5. Name three functions an operating system is responsible for.

Hardware and software requirements 1

Hardware

Hardware refers to the physical parts of a computer system such as the mouse, monitor, hard drive and processor. When any information system is being implemented it is essential that the correct hardware is selected or in place to meet the requirements of the system. In this section we will look at various hardware devices.

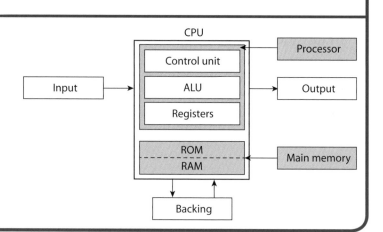

Input devices

- **Mouse:** used to move a pointer on a screen.
- **Keyboard:** used to key in data.
- **Microphone and soundcard**: used to capture sound.
- **Touchpad:** used on laptops to move a pointer round a screen.
- **Touch screen:** user touches parts of the screen to select icons.
- **Graphics tablet:** used to draw graphics onto a screen, using a stylus.
- **Scanner**: used to capture images or text from a paper document.
- **Digital camera and video recorder:** used to capture images and video.
- **Joystick:** used to move an icon or object round a screen. May be used in simulators or games.

Output devices

Printers

Two types of printers you will need to know about are **inkjet** and **laserjet**.

- **Inkjet printers:** cheap to buy (initial cost) but expensive to run (running cost). Inkjet printers use ink cartridges that squirt tiny droplets of quick-drying ink onto the paper.
- **Laserjet printers:** expensive to buy (initial cost) but cheaper to run (running cost). A laserjet uses a laser to make an image of electric charges. The image is then transferred onto paper using a powder called toner.

Display screens

The most common screen used today in computing is a TFT or LCD flat screen. Both are **low power**, and therefore **energy efficient**.

Other output devices

- **Speakers/headphones** with soundcard: used to output sound from a computer.
- **Flatbed plotter:** uses a pen to create an image on a horizontal sheet.
- **Digital projector:** for displaying images on a whiteboard, or to an audience.

EXAM TIP

Have a look around your classroom. How many input devices and output devices can you name?

Quick Test 36

1. Name three input devices.
2. What other device does a microphone need to work?
3. Why are LCD and TFT screens considered energy efficient?
4. What does a plotter use to create an image?
5. What type of printer is considered cheapest to run?

Hardware and software requirements 2

Processors

The processor is one of the most important bits of hardware inside a computer system. It is responsible for managing the **execution of programs**. The **clock speed** of a processor is one way the performance of the computer system is measured, and it is measured in **Hertz (Hz)**. This tells us how fast a processor is fetching and executing program instructions.

The typical clock speed of a processor in a laptop or desktop computer is between 2GHz and 3GHz. Smartphones have slower processors, and generally operate around 500MHz–1.5GHz.

The processor has three main components:

- **Control unit:** this part of the processor sends out signals to control the **fetching** and the **execution** of program instructions held in the main memory.

- **ALU (arithmetic and logic unit):** this performs all the **arithmetic** and **logic** functions within the processor.

- **Registers:** these are **temporary storage** locations on the processor chip.

Dual core and quad core processors

Processors were originally designed with one core. But today's computer systems can and sometimes need to use **dual core processors** such as AMD Phenom II X2, and Intel Core Duo.

More powerful systems make use of **quad core processors**, such as AMD Phenom II X4, and Intel's quad-core processors. The additional power in these types of processors is especially useful for **video editing**, **gaming** or **CAD** drawing where a lot of processor power is required.

Memory

Main memory is located inside the system unit and is used to store the programs and data being executed by the processor. It is made up of RAM and ROM.

RAM (random access memory)

RAM stores all instructions and data that are currently in use. If the power is lost, then the content of the RAM is also lost. In programs such as MS Word or games, a copy is loaded from the backing storage into RAM.

ROM (read only memory)

The programs contained in ROM can only be read by the processor, and cannot be written to. The contents of ROM remain in place after the power is switched off, and it contains important parts of the computers operating system, such as the **bootstrap loader**, which are essential for the computer to work.

Quick Test 37

1. What does a processor do?
2. What part of a processor sends out signals to control the fetching and the execution of program instructions?
3. What happens to data stored in RAM if the power is switched off?
4. What is the name of the part of the operating system that's stored in ROM?
5. What is the ALU responsible for within the processor?

Storage 1

All data and programs are stored permanently on backing **storage devices**. Some devices are built into a computer system and cannot be removed, like internal hard drives and internal RAM in a smartphone. Others can be external, like large capacity network hard drives. These would not be considered portable, however, unlike flash drives and CDs, which are small in physical size and portable.

Backing storage devices

Magnetic devices

Magnetic devices store data by coding it on to the magnetic coating of a disc. Hard discs are solid, rigid discs that can store upwards of 2TB of data. They can be written to many times.

Optical devices

Optical devices use a laser to read and write data that is coded onto the surface of the disc.

- **CD-ROM/DVD ROM:** holds data that can be read but not written. It is read only.
- **CD-R/DVD-R:** can be written to once. It can be read often but not re-written.
- **CD RW/DVD-RW:** can be written to many times.

Solid state

Solid state devices have no moving parts. USB flash drives and memory cards are solid state. Solid state hard drives are also installed in some laptops and consume less power than a standard magnetic hard drive, thus saving battery life. They are, however, quite expensive, and cannot hold as much data as a magnetic hard drive, but they are more robust and, because they have no moving parts, they are less likely to corrupt the data stored if the laptop falls or is knocked.

Capacity and speed of access

Two of the most important factors to consider with backing storage is how much data can they store and the speed of the data transfer. The table below gives a rough indication of the typical capacity and speeds of these devices.

Device	Typical capacity	Read/write speed
Magnetic hard disc	500 MB–4 TB	140 MB/s
Solid state hard disc	64 GB–512 GB	100 MB/s–600 MB/s
USB flash drive	4 GB–32 GB	14.65 MB/s
DVD-R/RW	4.7 GB (8.5 GB Dual Layer)	33.2 MB/s
CD-R/RW	700 MB	7.2 MB/s
Memory card	4 GB–64 GB	90 MB/s

Quick Test 38

1. What are backing storage devices used for?
2. Name an optical storage device.
3. What are two important factors to consider when looking at backing storage devices?
4. Name two benefits to using solid state hard drives.

Storage 2

Interfaces

An interface is required to connect a backing storage device or peripheral to the CPU. It is used to compensate for the differences in how they operate.

- **Differences in speed:** The processor of a computer operates at a much higher speed than a peripheral does. The interface is used to compensate for these differences.
- **Data conversion:** Data may be required to be converted from analogue to digital, or the voltage may need to be changed between a device and the computer.
- **Temporary storage:** Data may be required to be stored temporarily in an area of memory called a buffer, until it is ready to be used by the computer system.

Interface types

Different interface types have different rates at which they can transfer data from the device to the CPU. The table below will give you an idea of the difference in common interface transfer rates.

EXAM TIP

Try transferring photos from your smartphone using Bluetooth and then again using the USB cable. Note the difference in speed.

Interface	Data transfer rate	Time to transfer 1 GB of data
USB 2.0	480 Mbps	15 seconds
USB 3.0	5 Gbps	1.4 seconds
Bluetooth 3.0	24 Mbps	5 minutes
Firewire	800 Mbps	9.5 seconds
Thunderbolt	10 Gbps	0.7 seconds

Quick Test 39

1. What is an interface?
2. Name three things an interface is responsible for.
3. What is one common interface type?
4. Apart from data conversion, what else might need to be converted between a peripheral and a CPU?

Networking and connectivity

Types of networks

A computer network is where two or more computers are connected together. They allow users to share data, share peripherals and communicate. There are two types of networks you need to know about: **client server** and **peer-to-peer**.

Client server

A client server network has two types of computers called a **client** and a **server**.

- **Client:** the client is a workstation computer, like the one you use in school. It accesses the network resources provided by the server.
- **Server:** the server is a powerful computer that provides network resources. The server provides data and files that a client needs, e.g. word processing software, user files and access to the Internet. It is used as a central backing storage area for all the clients. This makes backing-up files easier than peer-to-peer networks.

Peer-to-peer

A peer-to-peer network is when the computers act as both client and server, and can share data and communicate with every other computer on the network. Each computer can access any of the others. If you set up a home network, it is most likely a peer-to-peer network.

Comparison	Client server	Peer-to-peer
Sharing resources	Managed by the server and provides clients with resources.	Each workstation makes its resources available.
Storage	Data stored centrally on the server.	No centralised storage. Each workstation stores its own data.
Type of environment	Businesses and organisations. Lots of users.	Trusted environment. Family home, small business.
Security	Server holds usernames and passwords. Login required to access user files.	Difficult to manage as no central management system. Individual usernames and passwords on workstations.

Media

Transmission media is the way in which data is able to transmit across a network. There are three main ways: **wired**, **optical** and **wireless**.

- **Wired:** a wired network uses cables to transmit data around the network. Twisted pair copper cable or coaxial cable is used. They have relatively fast connection speeds, are quite cheap and are used in many small businesses.
- **Optical:** fibre optic cables are used to send data at high speed through a network. The light forms an electromagnetic carrier wave that is modulated to carry information. They have very fast connection speeds compared to standard copper cabling, but are more expensive.
- **Wireless:** this is a common method used in homes and small business. Wireless is used to carry data around a network without the use of wires. It allows for freedom of movement, and is getting faster all the time. Wireless, however, could be considered a less secure way of transferring data than wired transmission.

Local versus cloud

Cloud storage is becoming a more popular way to use networks. Cloud storage is able to store data and resources remotely on a server that is attached to the Internet. Users can access their files and data anywhere there is an internet connection.

With a local network users can only get access to the server using a computer that is on that local network. This can be quite restricting.

Quick Test 40

1. What is a computer network?
2. What is one security benefit to using a client server network?
3. What environment is a peer-to-peer network used in?
4. Name three ways data is transmitted across a network.
5. What is cloud computing?

Network security

Security risks

There are many security risks associated with using networks and computer systems. While the use of networks has greatly improved global communication over the years, the risks associated with using them has grown. Criminals are always looking for new techniques to steal data and information from computer systems and networks.

Spyware

Spyware can capture information such as web browsing habits, e-mail messages, usernames and passwords, and credit card information.

Phishing

Phishing is a method used to try and get someone's username, password or personal details. Criminals send out emails that appear to come from legitimate sites such as PayPal, eBay, or banking institutions. The e-mails state that your information needs to be updated and ask you to enter your username and password by clicking on a link. Once clicked you are taken to a site that looks identical to the real website. You 'log in', enter your personal details, and the criminals have access to them.

Keylogging

Keylogging is a method of recording a user's keystrokes and recording them. The log can be saved as a file or sent to another machine over the Internet, allowing someone else to have access to everything typed on that computer, including passwords.

Online fraud and identity theft

Online fraud is when someone using online services has their information or money stolen. Rogue security software is a common method that fraudsters use online. Posing as a legitimate bank website or other trusted site, users put in their personal details thinking they are logging into a secure site. Their personal details and passwords are then sent to the fraudsters. This can even lead to identity theft.

Identity theft

Identity theft is a form of stealing someone's identity by having access to their personal information. Once this information, such as date of birth, mother's maiden name, bank account information, etc., is in the hands of criminals, they are able to make fake passports and identification, or take out credit in your name.

Denial of service attacks (DOS)

One of the most common attacks on computer networks is called a denial of service attack (DOS.) This is when hackers flood the network with useless requests that the server has to deal with. This in turn means that the server and network are unable to operate or manage legitimate requests. Websites such as Amazon, MasterCard and Visa have all been targeted this way in the past by hacker groups who wish to damage the companies' reputations.

EXAM TIP

Look online for recent viruses and DOS attacks that have happened to big companies.

Security precautions

EXAM TIP

Ask your Computing teacher what user privileges are installed on the school network. Does the teacher have different privileges to a pupil?

Security on networks is essential and access to user's files and confidential information must be protected. There are many ways in which data on a network is kept secure.

Passwords

Access to a network is usually by a **username** and **password**. Each user is given different access rights to the network, known as user privileges. In school, the network administrator would have full access to the network, and can install software and access all files. Pupils cannot do this, as they do not have access rights. Pupils usually only have access to the services they require to do their work, and no more.

Encryption

Encryption is a method of security where confidential data is encoded so that even if it is hacked into, the data is not of any use to the hackers. The data can only be decoded by a software key to turn it back into its original state. Encrypted hard drives and USB flash drives are becoming more common.

Biometrics

In today's technological age, we have to remember lots of passwords or PINs to access computer networks – from accessing our emails and social networking sites, to accessing files on our laptops and mobile phones.

Biometrics use physical traits to identify a person, such as a fingerprint, retina scan or voice recognition. It is a more secure way to access a network and is very difficult for someone else to replicate.

But this brings some concerns too. Biometric data is not changeable. If the unique human characteristics used for biometric access are compromised the affected person has no possibility of getting new ones issued.

Firewalls

A firewall is a program or hardware device that filters the data coming through the Internet connection into your private network or computer system. If an incoming piece of data does not match set criteria, then it does not get through the filters.

Use of security suites

Security suites such as Norton and McAfee are a collection of software utilities that protect a user's computer from viruses and other malware. Anti-virus and firewalls are usually the most common elements of a security suite. Other functions include:

- **Antispam:** stops spam email getting through.
- **Parental controls:** allow parents to limit the sites their children can access.
- **Password storage:** stores all user passwords in a secure format.
- **Backup:** allows for backup of files.
- **Tune up:** cleans the computer of old un-used files, cleans the registry and the Internet history.

Quick Test 41

1. Why is it important to have security on a network?
2. How is encoded data turned back into its original format?
3. What is one concern with the use of biometrics?
4. What is a firewall?
5. Name three features of a security suite.

Legal implications 1

Computer Misuse Act (1990)

This act is designed to make it illegal to hack into a computer system or to use a computer system for an illegal purpose. Under this act it is an offence to gain unauthorised access to a system or to make unauthorised modifications to software and files, e.g. writing and distributing viruses.

Modifying computer material

The Act defines this as:

- Interfering with a system so that it does not run properly.
- Making changes to the system to prevent others from accessing it.
- Making changes to software and data.

Data Protection Act (1998)

The Data Protection Act (1998) controls the **collection**, **storage** and **use** of **personal data** stored on manual and electronic systems.

There are three groups named in the act. These are: **data subjects**, **data controllers** and **data users**.

Data subjects

The individuals whose **data is stored** on a computer. They have the right to:

- see **personal** data
- **prevent** processing likely to cause damage or distress
- prevent processing for the purposes of **direct marketing** (junk mail)
- seek **compensation for damages**
- **correct, delete** and **destroy** incorrect data.

Data controllers

The people who **store** the data. Data controllers must:

- register with the **Data Protection Commissioner**
- apply for **permission** to store personal data on a computer
- state what data they want to keep, the **purpose** of it, and **who** is accessing it.

Data users

The people who **use** the information. Data users must follow the data protection principles listed below. All personal data should be:

- processed only if the individual **agrees** to it, if it is part of a **legal contract**, if it is essential to a **business transaction** or to the carrying out of public duties
- held for the **specified purpose**
- **accurate** and up-to-date
- **relevant**
- **adequate** for the purpose
- processed in accordance with the **rights of the subject**
- surrounded by **adequate security** such as passwords and/or encryption
- transferred only to countries outside the European Economic Area (EEA) that have **adequate security** measures.

Exceptions to the Act

If data is held by the police, security forces or the Inland Revenue, then access is denied.

EXAM TIP

Know the people involved with the Data Protection Act, and what their rights and responsibilities are.

Quick Test 42

1. What are two rights the customer has under the Data Protection Act?
2. What are the three groups connected with the Data Protection Act?
3. Which act makes it an offence to gain unauthorised access to a system?
4. In what circumstances are there exceptions to the Data Protection Act?

Legal implications 2

Copyright Designs and Patents Act (1988)

This act covers the illegal copying of published material such as images, text, video and music. It is illegal to do the following:

- Make **pirate** (unauthorised) copies of software.
- Run pirated software.
- Transmit software over network connections and copy it.
- Run **multiple copies** of software if only one copy was paid for.
- **Lend** or **sell** software to others without a **licence**.
- **Plagiarise** other people's work.

EXAM TIP

Make sure you get the name of this act correct.

Health and safety regulations

There are many health and safety regulations covering the workplace, and the use of information systems. The main ones are outlined below.

Lighting

Fluorescent lighting in a room can produce **glare** on computer monitors, and should not be used in a room with monitors. Windows can also produce glare, and monitors need to be positioned to avoid this.

Repetitive strain injury (RSI)

RSI is a condition that affects the muscles. Poor posture and continuous use of keyboards and mice can affect tendons and nerves in the arms, wrists and back. Improving posture can help prevent the disorder while stretches and strengthening exercises can help with recovery.

Eye strain

Eye strain can be caused by staring for long periods of time at a monitor. The eyes become dry and irritated over time. This can be prevented by the following:

- Adjusting the screen and the room lights to keep glare to a minimum.
- Avoiding any tendency to stare at the screen without blinking, as this can lead to dryness in the eyes.

Radiation

Computers, like all electrical instruments, emit extremely low frequency (ELF) radiation in very small amounts.

Seating

It is important to have a good posture when sitting at a computer. The chair must have an adjustable back and good lower-back support, as well as be adjustable in height.

Quick Test 43

1. Which act makes it illegal to run pirated software?
2. Name one health and safety issue when using an information system.
3. What can be done to avoid eye strain when using a monitor?
4. Why can't you lend or sell software to others without a licence?

Environmental impact

The energy a computer system consumes when it is in use contributes significantly to the environmental footprint of the company that made it. It also contributes significantly to your environmental footprint.

With global warming at the forefront of people's minds, companies must ensure that they are seen to be green, and **environmentally friendly**. There are several ways in which a company, organisation or individual user can reduce their carbon footprint, reduce the energy that they use, and dispose of any IT equipment that is no longer in use.

Energy use

Computer systems consume power. The amount of power that is consumed depends on the individual system, and the hardware inside the computer. High-end computer systems with the latest hardware will consume more power than an office computer system that uses low-end hardware. This of course has financial implications on any organisation using a lot of computer systems. Huge companies like Amazon and Google run hundreds of computer systems and servers and need to have strategies in place that help them consume less power.

Many manufacturers of computer systems have energy-saving techniques built in, such as ambient light sensors that automatically turn down the brightness of a monitor, to systems automatically going into standby mode if not in use after a set period of time. Individual users can also set their computers to save energy. Some of these ways are as follows:

- Use built-in power-saving features.
- Turn off the monitor instead of using a screensaver.
- Disable devices that are not needed, such as WiFi.
- Share hardware where appropriate.

EXAM TIP

Have a look at the power-saving options for your school or home computer. Are you wasting energy?

Carbon footprint

The environment has become an important subject and we are always being asked to do our bit to try to reduce our carbon footprint. There are several ways in which an organisation or individual can reduce their carbon footprint. By using energy-saving features on electronic equipment, we use less energy, and this will reduce our footprint. However, there are other ways we can do this, such as putting documents online rather than printing them out or sending emails rather than letters through the post. This will reduce not only the amount of paper being wasted, but will also contribute to less rubbish being produced and then disposed of. Eventually all this paper needs to be put into landfill.

Disposal of IT equipment

All computer equipment is classed as waste electrical and electronic equipment (WEEE) and must be disposed of in a correct manner. We cannot dispose of old IT equipment the same way we dispose of normal rubbish. Certain items requiring disposal are classed as **hazardous waste** and must be collected, transported and treated in accordance with Control of Substances Hazardous to Health (COSHH) guidelines. CRT monitors and acid batteries are examples of these materials. By disposing of or recycling IT equipment in the correct way, you can offset your carbon footprint. Every properly recycled computer system saves tons of CO_2 emissions.

Quick Test 44

1. What is one way you could reduce the energy a computer uses?
2. How can you reduce your carbon footprint?
3. Why must some IT equipment be disposed of in a correct and safe way?
4. Name one energy-saving technique some computers have built into them.

Quick test answers

Quick Test 1

1. Source code.
2. Assembly language.
3. Machine code.
4. The operating system.

Quick Test 2

1. String variables.
2. Boolean variables.
3. Type integer.
4. The float() function.
5. String values have quotes round them.

Quick Test 3

1. The print function.
2. It is a comment.
3. Console.
4. The int () function.
5. The float () function.

Quick Test 4

1. 5.75.
2. 1024.
3. −1.
4. 7.
5. 4.0.

Quick Test 5

1. Sequence.
2. Iteration.
3. Selection.
4. For loop.
5. print(round (Result, 4)).

Quick Test 6

1. The **if statement**.
2. The **elif clause**.

3. Python uses **nested if statements** to handle multiple conditions.
4. The operators are == (equality) and != (inequality).
5. Comparison operators can be combined using **and** and **or**.

Quick Test 7

1. For loop.
2. While loop.
3. For loop.
4. (1, 11).
5. False.

Quick Test 8

1. The sum() function.
2. String.
3. The math module.
4. Radians.
5. Pi and e.

Quick Test 9

1. 0 to 65535 (0 to $2^{16} - 1$).
2. The size of the mantissa.
3. Unicode allows the representation of a much large number of characters.
4. 256.

Quick Test 10

1. Processor busses.
2. Control bus.
3. Connecting to a monitor.
4. USB.

Quick Test 11

1. The Python equivalent would be:

```
For index in range(1, 11):
print(index)
```

2. **END WHILE** and **END FOR** statements are not necessary in Python because the end of an indented section of code indicates the end of the loop.

3. The code fragment could be expressed as follows:

```
SEND "Enter Y or N" TO DISPLAY
RECEIVE response FROM KEYBOARD
WHILE (response ≠ "Y") AND (response ≠ "N") DO
 SEND "You must enter Y or N" TO DISPLAY
 RECEIVE response FROM KEYBOARD
END WHILE
```

4. `if… elif…`

5. `response = input("Enter Y or N: ").`

Quick Test 12

1.
```
while (response != "Y") and (response != "N"):
        print("Response must be Y or N")
        response = input("Enter Y or N: ")
```

2.
```
mcount = 0
fcount = 0
for index in range (0,9):
        gender = input("Enter gender (M or F): ")
        height = int(input("Enter height (cm): "))
        weight = int(input("Enter weight (kg): "))

        if (gender == 'M') and (height > 160) and (weight > 60):
          mcount = mcount + 1
        elif (gender == 'F') and (height > 150) and (weight > 50):
           fcount = fcount + 1

        print("")
print("The number of males with height > 160 and
weight > 60 is: ", mcount)
print("The number of females with height > 160 and weight > 60 is:
", fcount)
```

Quick Test 13

1. Integer
2. Float
3. Integer
4. Float

Quick Test 14

1. True.
2. False.
3. `phrase = "Hello World"`
4. `print(len('Hello World'))`

Quick Test 15

1. Syntax error.
2. Run-time error.
3. Logic error.
4. During compilation or interpretation.
5. If the program appears to run successfully but the output is incorrect.

Quick Test 16

1. Exceptional data.
2. Extreme data.
3. Exceptional data.
4. Extreme data.

Quick Test 17

1. Test plan.
2. Test log.
3. It should be removed.
4. Anyone reading them should be a programmer and familiar with the basic concepts.
5. Program name/id, programmer's name, date written.

Quick Test 18

1. The Python Shell and the Editing Window.
2. Syntax highlighting.
3. Choose Run and then Run Module from the menu.

Quick Test 19

1. Python uses a text-based environment. App Inventor uses a graphical environment that allows programs to be constructed from blocks.
2. Massachusetts Institute of Technology (MIT).
3. On an Android phone or on an emulator supplied with the package.
4. The designer and the blocks editor.
5. Via USB or WiFi.

Quick Test 20

1. The if block executes a sequence of instructions if a specified condition is true. It does nothing if the specified condition is False.
2. The ifelse block executes one sequence of instructions if a specified condition is true and a different sequence of instructions if the condition is false.
3. Complex selections are handled by nested ifelse blocks.

Quick Test 21

1. The loop counter variable, start value, final value and step size.
2. For range block.
3. While block.
4. Any value, positive or negative.

Quick Test 22

1. Methods.
2. Boolean.
3. Variables are defined by selecting the **def variable as** block under **Built-In / Definition** in the Blocks Editor.
4. In the Math block group.

Quick Test 23

1. Floor returns the greatest integer that is less than or equal to the given number. Round returns the integer closest to the given number.
2. It will be rounded to the nearest even integer.
3. Degrees.

Quick Test 24

1. Reduced instruction set computer (RISC).
2. Lexical analysis.
3. False. Compilers and Interpreters can exist for the same language.
4. Optimisation.

Quick Test 25

1. The interpreter never has access to the whole program – it processes the program line by line.
2. Intermediate code or Bytecode.
3. A computer program that emulates a real machine.
4. If changes are made to the program they can be tested immediately without having to wait for the program to be recompiled.

Quick Test 26

1. A combination of hardware and software that stores information that people can access and manipulate.
2. Data duplication and data inconsistency.
3. A database made up of multiple linked tables.
4. It is a unique item of data used to identify a row.
5. Field size is the maximum size a field can hold. Field range is the range of data a field will accept.

Quick Test 27

1. A collection of webpages and hyperlinks.
2. Internal points to a part of the same page or different page on the same site. External points to another website.
3. Uniform resource locator.
4. Linear, hierarchal or web.

Quick Test 28

1. GUI.
2. To be clearly organised, free from clutter and allow users to locate information.
3. It looks more professional.
4. Using icons, navigation bars or menus.

Quick Test 29

1. MP3.
2. To transfer over a network faster and to reduce the file size.
3. Lossless.
4. Lossy.
5. RTF.

Quick Test 30

1. MPEG.
2. 24 bit.
3. 1 or 0.
4. BMP, JPEG, GIF.

Quick Test 31

1. 256.
2. Amount of pixels in an image. DPI.
3. 24 bit.
4. The number of bits to store a sound.
5. The files are very large in size, and take up lots of storage.

Quick Test 32

1. The system does what it was designed to do.
2. Expert and novice.
3. So that there are no serious problems with using the system.
4. Graphical user interface consisting of icons and a pointing device, usually a mouse.

Quick Test 33

1. High-level programming language that is interpreted by another program.
2. Server side and client side.
3. It is used by web authors to allow them to create dynamic and interactive web content.
4. They are used for the processing and the presentation of text.

Quick Test 34

1. To make sure that it is working for the purpose it was intended for.
2. To ensure the user can navigate around a system.
3. Any two: check there are no broken links or hyperlinks; check for smooth transitions between screens; check all hyperlinks work correctly; check all links within the application work.
4. What each element of the user interface should do.
5. Any two: check the layout matches the design; check that the spelling is correct; check scroll functions, audio and video clips run without problems; check that the buttons of the page work; check the texts, fonts, colours and sizes match the original design.

Quick Test 35

1. Super computer, laptop, tablet, smartphone, desktop.
2. Same specification as desktop, lighter, portable, prices coming down.
3. Solid state.
4. Size and functionality.
5. Error reporting, managing programs, performing input and output, saving and loading files, provides HCI.

Quick Test 36

1. Any answer from bullet list on input devices.
2. Soundcard.
3. They are low power.
4. A pen.
5. LaserJet.

Quick Test 37

1. It is responsible for managing the execution of programs.
2. Control unit.
3. It is lost.
4. Bootstrap loader.
5. Arithmetic and logic functions.

Quick test 38

1. To permanently store data and programs.
2. CDR/RW DVDR/RW.
3. Capacity, access speeds, portability.
4. Robust, consume less energy.

Quick Test 39

1. It connects a backing storage device or peripheral to the CPU.
2. Data conversion, temporary storage, compensate for different speeds.
3. USB, Bluetooth, Firewire, Thunderbolt.
4. Voltage.

Quick Test 40

1. Two or more computers connected together.
2. Usernames and passwords stored on server.
3. Trusted.
4. Wired, optical and wireless.
5. They are able to store data and resources remotely on a server that is attached to the Internet.

Quick test 41

1. To protect users files and confidential information.
2. Using a software key.
3. The data is not changeable.
4. Program or hardware device that filters the data coming through the Internet connection into your private network or computer system.
5. Antispam, parental controls, password storage, backup, tune up, anti-virus, firewall.

Quick Test 42

1. To see personal data; prevent processing likely to cause damage or distress; prevent processing for the purposes of direct marketing; to seek compensation for damages; to correct, delete and destroy incorrect data.
2. Data subjects, data controllers and data users.
3. Computer Misuse Act.
4. If data is held by the police, security forces or the Inland Revenue.

Quick Test 43

1. Copyright Design and Patents Act.
2. Seating, radiation, lighting, eye strain, RSI.
3. Adjusting the screen and the room lights, avoiding any tendency to stare at the screen without blinking.
4. Because it breaks the Copyright Design and Patents Act.

Quick Test 44

1. Use built-in power saving features; turn off the monitor instead of using a screensaver; disable devices that are not needed; share hardware where appropriate.
2. Put documents online instead of printing them; use any power saving features; recycle correctly.
3. Some IT equipment can be hazardous to health.
4. Ambient light sensors, automatic standby.